COMMON SENSE DISCIPLINE

DR. ROGER ALLEN AND RON ROSE

COMMON SENSE DISCIPLINE

WHAT TO SAY AND DO WHEN KIDS NEED HELP

SD

Sweet Publishing
Ft. Worth, Texas
G.R. Welch Ltd., Canada

COMMON SENSE DISCIPLINE

What To Say and Do When Kids Need Help

Copyright ©1986 by Sweet Publishing,
3934 Sandshell, Fort Worth, Texas 76137-2403

Library of Congress Card Catalog Number 86-061522

ISBN 0-8344-0135-5

10   9   8   7   6   5   4   3   2   1

In honor of the love my parents gave me

and dedicated

to the loving and lasting memory

of my father who taught me much

by what he chose neither to say nor do

when others acted irresponsibly.

Acknowledgements

This book would not have been possible without the guidance of two people who first introduced me to the practical aspects of child care work: Myron Beard, Ph.D., of San Antonio and Melvin Klement of New Dominion School, Dillwyn, Virginia. I will never be able to thank them enough for their advice and sensitivity.

In Tyler, several bookstore managers initially encouraged me to publish this, including Michael Burp, Paul Herman, Trudy Richardson and Ann Sefrna. Joan Hallmark of Station KLTV, Robert Main and Dan Gresham have helped me through the media. Phil Hook and Gary Lesniewski of Radio KVNE provided their support. My friend Brad Spradlin was a continual listening ear. William Stanton, M.D. and Brian Walker offered useful suggestions. Gail Wise typed most of the manuscript for this book with an eagerness that never seemed to fail. My publisher, Byron Williamson, has worked under a tight schedule to produce this edition. Ron Rose has made an important contribution to this book, especially the sections concerning teenagers and sexuality. Kolle and Dot-Dot showered Lane with their love while Kathy and I worked late. Chris Mock was a special help. For all of you, I am thankful.

But most of all, for the talents which make my work possible and permit me to provide for my family while helping others, I thank God.

Roger B. Allen, Ph.D.
Tyler, TX

Foreword

Ever since I wrote *Kids Say the Darndest Things*, people have been sending me funny stories about children. One of them concerns a little boy standing on his porch crying and rubbing his backside. When a kindly old gentleman asked what was the trouble, the youngster replied, "My daddy lost his psychology book, and now he's using common sense."

I am excited about this book, *Common Sense Discipline*, because it is the practical approach to parenting that is exactly what moms and dads need.

Perhaps more now than at any period in history the fiber of family life is in danger of being torn to shreds. Collapsing family life leads to sick children, who become sick adults, who create a sick nation.

If parents would follow the recommendations in this book, I believe our families would be stronger and safer. It is filled with words of wisdom and encourages parents to trust themselves and use common sense.

I like it.

Art Linkletter

Introduction

Rearing children is one of the least appreciated and most underpaid jobs you'll ever have. (In fact, it'll cost you a fortune.) When you're working hardest, you may be criticized most. Someone is always looking for someone to blame when a child goes wrong. Parents and teachers, for that matter, have all the responsibility, but little preparation and training. While you may have been taught Chaucer and calculus in school, you probably received little, if any, on-the-job training to prepare you for children. No matter how hard you work, how much overtime you put in, someone won't like what you do. Frequently that critic is the very kid you're working so hard to raise responsibly. Parents and teachers get no respect.

This book is for parents and teachers who want more information for helping their children grow to be responsible adults. It answers the questions I hear most frequently at parents' and teachers' workshops. It helps parents develop their own style, a common sense style, that sets a clear, confident course into the future while releasing parents of fear and doubt.

If this is your first lap around the track with kids, then know that the training is just beginning. If you already have responsibility for several children, you know how important endurance and strategy are. Frustrations creep in because we never seem to be as good at parenting as we want to be. This book will help you start right, keep it up, and develop your best game plan for each child.

Since 1968 I've been working with families from all walks of life, trying to help them find solutions to their problems. Their kids have ranged from normal, ordinary kids to those with severe emotional handicaps. Some were visually impaired; others had multiple handicaps.

Their parents ranged from Christian to heretic, well-educated to illiterate, rich to poor, liberal to conservative. The common dream of all those parents was a driving desire to be better parents. It's not an easy job, but few things worthwhile are easy.

The Bible is full of stories of parents who faced tough times. Can't you imagine Eve's anguish, "Where did we go wrong with Cain?" At a high point in his life, Job saw his family and fortune wiped out. That makes any mid-life crisis look pale by comparison. Certainly Jesus' parents must have provided all the right kinds of guidance and supervision, yet they didn't always understand what was going on in his mind (Luke 2:50). Just when things seemed to be looking best for Jesus, he was killed by an ungrateful mob. Do you suppose Mary ever said, "If only I had..."?

You're not alone if you've found kids to be a tough course of study. If your baby was easy—never had colic, never got fussy, and started sleeping through the night at age two weeks — congratulations! You were fortunate. But if your baby cried a lot, got sick easily, and nothing you did seemed to work, this book's for you.

Parents who have had an easy time of it will never understand what the rest of us go through!

If you've had trouble with your child, I know the pain you have felt. If your preschool child has scared you and made you wonder what sort of adult he's going to be, I've heard your story. If your teenager is sullen, disobedient, sassy and disrespectful, you are not alone.

Whether you're a novice or an old hand at teaching, you'll discover some useful tips for your classroom here.

We'll talk about helping students focus on their studies by simply rephrasing our instructions. Wouldn't it be nice to solve almost all of your behavior problems in the classroom without referring students to the office? We'll talk about how you can accomplish that objective. If you're a parent as well as a teacher, you'll find some welcomed suggestions for your work with children.

If you are looking for some common sense help with your kids, read on!

CONTENTS

12 RULES AND RESOURCES

1

Basics of Common
Sense Discipline

"Hi, my name is Ron, and my dad was an alcoholic."

It's a humbling experience, being raised with an alcoholic father. For years I tried to protect our family secret. During grade school I was embarrassed and ashamed, but in junior high I turned angry and resentful. I finally got to the point where I hated his bottle, I hated his slurred speech, and I hated him. The more I expressed my bitterness, the more he drank. Why couldn't he just stop? For 25 years Dad was an unconfessed alcoholic, and the wall between us grew higher and wider.

Until 1978 I was convinced that Dad had taught me nothing, that I had grown up cheated out of time and wisdom. Then, the impossible happened! Dad checked himself into a treatment center, spent 35 days learning to be sober, and never drank again. The next four years were spent tearing down the wall between us.

But it wasn't until my dad died that I finally realized God had used the 25 "wasted" years to teach Dad, and me, some pretty important lessons about life. At Dad's funeral I spoke about his life and the lessons it taught me.

Lesson #1: There are no perfect parents. There never has been nor will there ever be a perfect parent. Many well-meaning people spend a lifetime worrying about saying and doing the right things. Their dominant feeling in life is frustration because they're never right enough or good enough.

Have you noticed that there are no perfect parents described in the Bible? They messed up — some of them royally. God created each of us to be unique and individual. He gave us principles to live by, and then he asked us to become the parents we were meant to be. We will not all be the same. There is no perfect mold.

Lesson #2: Don't freeze-frame others. Dad took 8mm movies as we were growing up. On the evening of his funeral we watched those films. We cried a lot, and we laughed a lot.

We all have a tendency to freeze-frame, or label, people. Dad was an "alcoholic." This person's "funny," that one's "smart," this kid's a "discipline problem." It's almost like trapping their image in a picture and assuming they will stay that way all their lives. I don't want people to trap me the way I used to be. I need the freedom to change and so do kids. And so did Dad.

Lesson #3: Always count your options. Dad spent years trapped in alcoholism. After he finally realized he had options, he broke free.

We are only trapped when we feel as if we have no choice. At times life seems hopeless, and options vanish. But those times are only temporary. I believe there are always options, even when we don't yet see them.

This book is designed to help you discover options where you may feel trapped. It will help you choose appropriate options in teaching your children about life — that's what discipline is all about. P.S. Thanks, Dad, for the lessons.

To begin with we need to look at some basic principles.

THE MEANING OF DISCIPLINE

Some people think that "discipline" means punishment. That's obvious when we hear a parent tell a child, "You better straighten up or I'm going to lay some discipline on you." What he really means is, "Stop or you're going to get it." However, the English word "discipline" comes from the Latin "disciplina" which means instruction. When we discipline we teach; we prepare our children for life.

Walter Brueggemann in his commentary on Genesis points out an interesting set of contrasts which God employed in disciplining his first children:

> Permission matched with prohibition;
> Protection matched with punishment.
> Genesis 2 & 3

It's as if God tells Adam and Eve, "You can do almost anything you want with this exception. So long as you obey me you'll be well cared for and happy. But break these rules and you'll be punished." Unfortunately, Adam and Eve disobeyed, and they were punished by being banished from the garden of God's protection.

Ever since the garden, God has been preparing us for life in heaven, and he is still giving permission, prohibition, protection and punishment to keep us on our toes.

Throughout the Bible we see these themes repeated over and over. "This you can do, this you can't." So long as you act responsibly and do what God says, you'll be all right. Break his laws and you'll suffer the consequences. That's how God deals with his children. In Moses' sermon text of Deuteronomy, God is portrayed as a father who leads, humbles and tests his children, disciplining them to see what's in their heart (Deuteronomy 8:1-5). God was preparing his children for life.

Jesus' followers were called "disciples" because their whole lives were invested in learning from Jesus. If you want to effectively discipline (teach) your child, think of discipline as preparation for living a grown-up life.

Instead of asking, "What's the best way to discipline my child?" we might do better by asking, "How can I teach my child to become a responsible adult in the same way God is teaching me?"

THE COMMON SENSE GOAL

Common sense will help us to ask the right questions, and God will lead us in the right direction. However, there will be times when we will feel lost and distracted. There are even times when we all feel like total failures. The frustration of feeling trapped and lost can take its toll on any of us. We could all use a little help in the trenches.

The number one concern of parents across this nation is discipline. Nothing will help you enjoy the adventure of parenting more than developing a personal discipline plan that really works.

The goal of Common Sense Discipline is to help concerned parents and teachers raise resourceful children who have learned to be responsible adults. This is a worthy goal, but it takes time, and some parents quit before they get started!

The Common Sense Discipline Chart on the next page describes the process of helping your child become respon-

Common Sense Discipline Chart 1

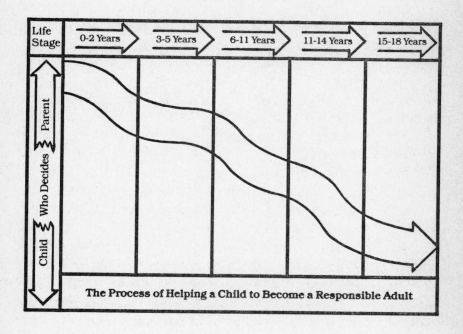

Life Stage	0-2 Years	3-5 Years	6-11 Years	11-14 Years	15-18 Years

Who Decides — Parent ⇕ Child

The Process of Helping a Child to Become a Responsible Adult

sible. It is apparent that both parent and child will have to travel this pathway together. As the kids grow older, they are encouraged to make their own decisions and control their own behavior. It's like teaching your child to ride a bicycle. At first you hold the bike steady and run alongside for at least a thousand miles. As your child gets his balance, you turn loose for a while. Then after dozens of scraped knees and a few minor emergencies, your child becomes a Red Cross certified safe bicycle rider, as you look on with a revived sense of pride.

Using the Discipline Chart as a guide, let's consider the issue of school.

During the 0-2 years parents will make all the decisions for the children. The only exceptions are the child's selection of toys to play with.

During the 3-5 years parents will make the majority of decisions for children, especially in the health and safety areas. So, in the second column we might imagine a parent who decides whether or not her child goes to day care, Sunday School or no pre-school at all. That decision is completely up to the parent. Your child's decisions might be what to take to "show and tell." When your four-year-old makes a request, ask yourself: "Should I decide this, or should he decide?"

While your child is 6-11 years old you'll still want to make most of the major decisions about school. But, only your child can make the decisions about how he *relates* to school. During this time I encourage parents to permit children to decide what clothes to wear to school. Getting a little chilly because he wore a short-sleeved shirt instead of a long-sleeved shirt will cause him to make a better decision next time. As I was growing up, I often wondered why Mother would say, "Roger, put on your coat" when *she* got cold. How about you?

During the 11-14 years these words are appropriate: "Homework is now your responsibility. If you need help, I'll help, *if I can*. If your grades start to suffer, then your activities will be cut back, and you'll have a mandatory study time."

In the years from 15-18 parents with Common Sense Discipline really make very few decisions for their teens. Their teens still mess it up, but they get good advice and fix it up. They practice being responsible.

I am fairly strict when it comes to providing structure that children need. But, like removing braces once the teeth are straight, there comes a time when the structure has to be gradually and carefully removed. It's just good common sense to do it.

Throughout this book I'll refer to the Discipline Chart to point out appropriate discipline methods. I will also use the chart to reflect on how difficult it is, at times, for parents to let the kids take responsibility for their own decisions.

SIX WAYS TO COMMUNICATE LOVE

In order to be the parent God wants us to be, we must know how to both love and discipline our kids. There are at least six ways to communicate love and discipline at the same time. I believe that understanding and using these options will help us be most effective with our kids:

1. Real life experiences
2. The examples of others or modeling
3. Opportunities to discover
4. Questions and reflecting
5. Punishment
6. Incentives

Note that punishment is included as one of several kinds of love messages. Ironically, while it's not the kind most parents would like to use, it's the only message some kids get. Let's talk about all six options.

Real Life Experiences

Life's a great teacher, isn't it? It doesn't take long to find out what happens when you write checks without concern for how much money is in your account. The result can be devastating and embarrassing. Many of life's lessons hurt; others are absolutely delightful, like learning how to ride a bike, finally cooking a meal that is all ready at the right time or discovering something new about the people you love.

Sometimes it helps to be told "how" before we try, as when God instructed Moses before he built the Tabernacle. Sometimes it helps to learn on your own and make your own mistakes because what works best for others may not be what works best for you.

Then there are times when, just like Jonah, we know what we should do, we just don't want to do it. Most of us remember our parents telling us to think ahead, save for the future and make various kinds of preparations, yet we often failed to learn those lessons until we got caught short.

Allowing children to experience life for themselves, both the good and the bad, enables them to learn important lessons for themselves and reinforce your love for them.

Examples or Modeling

Children learn a lot from watching others. Sometimes they learn from the strengths of others and sometimes from the weaknesses of others. We've all seen children trying to walk like their daddy, make friends like their mother and yell like someone down the street. "Monkey see, monkey do" is the hallmark of all small children.

Within the first few months of life children learn that your actions will always speak louder than words, though your words can say plenty. Be sure that what you say and do in front of your children teaches the kinds of lessons you want. That doesn't mean perfection in front of the kids. After all, who among us can be perfect all the time? The key is to admit failure and keep trying.

One father complained to me that his son was rude and ill-mannered toward his mother. When I saw the family together it was plain to see that the boy learned rudeness from the way his father treated his mother. If you resort to saying, "Do as I say and not as I do," then your words become cheap and your life powerless.

How soon do children start modeling the actions of those around them? Well, I can tell you about a funny incident that my wife, Kathy, pointed out to me.

"Roger, you know that funny way you curl your little finger when you hold a cup of tea? Watch how Lane holds his orange juice glass at breakfast tomorrow."

Lane was two years old then. Sure enough, he held his hand the same way I did, purposefully curling his little finger. I even caught him looking at the way I held my knife and fork while he tried to copy me.

Don't underestimate modeling as an effective communicator of love.

Opportunity to Discover

Once when our son Lane was four years old, we were sitting by a shallow fountain in the center of a shopping mall. Lane had a small boat that he was pushing around the circular pool. Soon another little boy about Lane's age came over, and they began taking turns with the boat. While the other boy was pushing the boat through the water, Lane decided to get on the concrete ledge that went all the way around the fountain. This ledge was about one foot wide and two feet off the mall's floor. I was tempted to tell him to get down because he might slip, but then I thought this might give us the opportunity for him to learn a useful lesson. Besides, walking around the ledge of a fountain looked like fun (I would have enjoyed doing it myself, but I have far too much dignity to have that much fun).

I'll have to admit I felt some risk in what Lane was doing. The ledge was concrete, and there were some slippery places on it where the water had splashed. So I asked myself, "What's the worst thing that's likely to happen?"

Well, the worst thing was that he might slip and bump his head.

Then I thought about what would happen if I told him, "No, you can't do that. Get down, come here, etc." We would immediately have had a confrontation; Lane would have begged me to let him continue, giving me endless reassurances that he would be careful.

While I didn't think it was likely he would have a bad fall, there was a real possibility that he might fall in and get soaked. Fortunately, it was a warm day, and Lane was wearing shorts, so getting wet wasn't a problem. I decided that if he did fall, he would learn a lesson that would probably last the rest of his life. Besides, if he didn't get up on that fountain this time, it was inevitable that he probably would on some future fountain, on some future day, just to prove that he could do it. So I let him walk around the ledge. Besides, kids love fountains, and he was only doing a perfectly natural thing for a kid.

Well, Lane didn't fall in. He jumped in! Later a man who had been watching everything from the other side of the fountain told me that it was obvious when Lane got the idea.

"You could just see it written all over his face, and he just squatted down and jumped in," the man said.

In all fairness to Lane, his version was that he was about to slip, and rather than lose his balance and fall, he chose to jump.

Lane came out of the water in near panic. Naturally his first concern was whether or not I was mad. How could I be when I saw it coming and accepted the risk?

"Are you okay?"

He nodded.

"That was really something, wasn't it?"

He nodded again.

Now, there are many good parents who would have "put their foot down" and told their child to get off that ledge. Some kids would obey immediately and that's that, but there are many good children who, upon hearing such a statement, would have firmly decided, "The first chance I get, I will get on that ledge...only when Mom or Dad aren't around."

Since that time, Lane and I have been back to that mall dozens of times. The first time back, about a week after he fell/jumped in, Lane glanced over at the fountain with a funny look on his face.

"Remember the time you fell in?" I asked. Of course, he did; he nodded.

"That was really something, wasn't it?" And he looked up and saw that I was only kidding, so he grinned. But Lane has never asked or even tried to climb back on the fountain. He's not afraid of it, and he doesn't walk far away from it.

What do you suppose our trips to the mall would have been like if I had not let him explore the ledge? One lesson learned is always better than one confrontation after another.

Most of us have had the experience of saying, "Let me do it by myself," or, "Let me figure out my own way, will you?" When parents and teachers allow and even encourage children to explore safe ways of doing new things, we provide them the opportunity to make useful and lasting discoveries. It's a great way to learn, given the right circumstances.

Questioning and Reflecting

While "discovery" allows learning by exploring, "questioning and reflecting" allow kids to learn by asking. And kids ask lots of questions, don't they?

Questions aren't always for the purpose of getting information. Sometimes they're intended to show us what a child is thinking, and at other times they are asked to get our attention. Have you ever heard questions like these:

- ☐ Are we there yet?
- ☐ Why can't I unburn my finger?
- ☐ How did you know it was me?
- ☐ How many bites of this stuff do I have to eat?
- ☐ Can you read that story again?
- ☐ Why do leaves fall off trees—do they get rusty?
- ☐ How come my reflection is left-handed?
- ☐ Can we have just one, please?
- ☐ Why don't you just get more money from the bank?
- ☐ What's eternity mean?

Questions do get our attention. But, you can have too much of a good thing. Sometimes this questioning routine will go on until someone gets tired and angry (somewhere between question number three and number ten). Then in frustration a typical parent will say, "Just because!" "Go ask Dad!" "That's enough, go look it up for yourself!" "That's enough, I don't want to hear another word!"

How to Use Questions. The next time a child asks you three questions in a row, you might pretend you are playing a child's version of "20 Questions." Instead of responding to question number four too readily, it might be useful to think about what's going on and how you could use this situation as a teaching opportunity. You could shift gears and say something like, "Hmm, that's a good question. I bet if you stop and think about it you can come up with the answer yourself." Or, "What do you think the answer could be?"

In one family I worked with, Dad liked to tell his kids (actually "order his kids" would better describe it), "Go look it up yourself." His motivation was to encourage his children to become resourceful and more independent. Unfortunately, he accomplished just the opposite by the sarcastic way he responded to their questions. Soon they didn't bother to ask him anything of importance out of fear that he would reject them.

I wonder what would have happened to that father's relationship with his children if the next time he was asked, "Dad, how come such and such——" he answered with, "That's a good question. Let's look it up together." He could have used the child's question as an opportunity to explain ways of finding solutions by saying something like, "Let's see, the best place to find out the meaning of a word is in the dictionary. The best place to find out more about those words is in an encyclopedia. Let's see if this one has it. Now, how is that word spelled?" And so his child would spell the word for him. "Okay, this book is in alphabetical order, so we use it like this," and the child learns a useful lesson.

If the question is about life, it's a great opportunity to discuss personal beliefs and values. These times can become significant memories for the kids. Notice that questions can be very useful in helping us invest our time in our children's lives. Questions are a natural to show we care.

Teaching with Reflection. Reflecting is a slightly different form of questioning. Instead of asking for information the child doesn't know, the child is asking the parent/ teacher to confirm that his own thinking is right. You've probably noticed that some children will come up and say, "Did you know that ——" when the "know that" concept is as plain as the nose on your face. But, for your child, it may be a brand new discovery.

Lane likes to ask me, "Dad, did you know it's raining?" when I've just come in from being soaked. You could respond with, "Sure, kid, even a moron knows that," and you'll probably never be bothered by that child's curiosity again. Or you could say, "Yes, that's really neat. Why do you suppose it does that?" Then your child would have a chance to discuss with you his discovery and to think more about it. So the next time your child asks, "Where does the sun go at night?" or "What's the biggest number in the world?" you might want to think about *how* to answer before you do.

Punishment

No question about it, children feel secure when they know the limits. Punishment for going beyond the limits can be a reminder that they are loved and cared for. Punishment usually takes one of two forms: either pain (such as spanking) or penalties (such as fines or restrictions like grounding).

Spanking. Punishment, in the form of pain, works best with young children, usually before they reach the third or fourth grade. Even then, spanking is an "iffy" proposition. Many times parents will choose to spank out of their own frustration. To be most effective, spanking should be used as a reaction to a major problem. If we aren't careful, it can be like using the emergency brake on your car when all you need to do is slow down for a stop sign. It doesn't make much sense to wear out your emergency brake when you can slow things down easier by using the regular brakes. The same goes for spanking. It doesn't make much sense to spank for minor problems when we can probably help children act better with more appropriate kinds of discipline.

I think it's best to reserve spanking for open defiance and rebellious behavior in children roughly 2-10 years of age. Defiance and rebellion are deliberate challenges to a parent's authority so it's time to step in and take prompt action. Also I might use spanking with very small children, about 2-4 years-old who violate safety rules like running into the street or sticking things into electrical outlets. When a child is too young to reason with or understand other kinds of punishment, I don't want to "discuss" unsafe behavior, I just want it to stop. Spanking may reduce misbehavior but won't teach the correct behavior. This is why spanking is largely ineffective in teaching our children about life and love.

Spanking Older Kids. After children reach the third or fourth grade, spanking becomes largely ineffective because of the increased padding in most children's rear ends.

Using spanking for minor problems is like using a chain saw to build a picture frame. It may work, but you'll probably do more than you wanted to, and frequently it won't fit together like you intended it to. If you decide to spank, before you begin decide whether to use one, two or three swats. Tell your child, "I'm going to give you 1-3 swats," and then get it over with.

I know some parents who made their son pull his jeans down when they spanked him in order to cause more pain. That seems downright mean to me and probably resulted in the boy feeling antagonistic toward his parents. In the same way, it's unwise to keep spanking until your child starts to scream and cry. Some children, out of spite or pride or hurt, will do anything to avoid crying. And if you keep spanking until they cry you may risk child abuse.

Paddling. I've heard some people suggest using a paddle instead of your hand because a child needs to associate your hands with hugging and holding, not inflicting pain. While hands do need to be associated with holding and hugging, to assume a child will come to fear hands because they occasionally spank makes about as much sense as thinking a child will come to fear cooked food because he was once burned by a stove.

Frankly, I don't care for paddles because a child is likely to see them for what they are, weapons of punishment. I don't think parents need to be in the business of using weapons. Using your hand is one thing, but using a belt or paddle because it hurts more seems unreasonable to me. If you're a principal in a school and paddlings are approved by your district, I encourage you to use them cautiously. Remember, the purpose of spanking is to discipline the child, not relieve the frustration of the parent or teacher. Doesn't that make sense?

Punishment is anything which is unpleasant to a child that comes as a result of that child's actions. Physical pain, such as spanking, may not be all that unpleasant, especially if being sent to the principal's office gets a student out of a particularly unpleasant class. Think back to when you were a kid. What one of us by the fifth grade wouldn't have preferred a quick spanking rather than being grounded for an entire week? The sting of a spanking rarely lasts for more than 15 minutes unless you abuse a child, but take away an allowance or ground a child for a week and the punishment seems like forever.

Potential Problems. Punishment often fails to teach desirable actions; it only suppresses an action. But if a child is running into the street, then all you want to do is to stop that action, so punishment may be appropriate. However, punishment does have some built-in problems.

Resentment - Punishment can result in resentment by both child and parent. If the punishment you administer doesn't relate to the behavior that took place, you run the risk of the child becoming resentful. For example, spanking a child for marking on a wall has nothing to do with that behavior. Or spanking one child for hitting another child makes little sense when the lesson you want the child to learn is to avoid hitting. When the punishment doesn't make sense, resentment is likely.

Backlash - One of the problems with strong punishment, especially spanking, is its potential to backfire on us, especially if we have a so-called "strong-willed" child. Kathy and I learned early with Lane that spanking him might stop unwanted behavior temporarily, but later he would do it again and again just to defy us. So, be careful!

Overkill/Child Abuse - All too often child abuse begins as punishment that gets out of hand. A parent tends to become desensitized to spanking, and so does the child. Gradually, like a person who develops resistance to a particular kind of medication through repeated use, it takes more and more to do the job. That's why it's especially important that, if you choose to spank, you decide ahead of time to use only one to three swats to avoid the punishment getting out of hand. Making this simple decision will provide immediate help.

Defeatism - Finally, if you need further reason to consider using other forms of discipline than punishment, think about this: Chris is always getting punished, excessively punished. He used to rebel and fight. Now, he is just worried and depressed. He feels that nothing he does is worthwhile and that he gets punished no matter what he does. Chris has now given up on everything—"Why try?"

Children who stop trying soon feel hopeless and helpless. Cutting off children's initiative through defeatism is like cutting off their emotional air. It's a cruel form of suffocation because children live on while their spirits die bit by bit.

Remember, the main thing children learn from punishment is what not to do instead of what to do. It takes caution and care to make it work right.

Incentives

An incentive is anything that encourages or reinforces continual actions or attitudes. Incentives tell us how we're cared for on a daily basis. Some of the typical incentives we are familiar with are paychecks, bonuses and various company "perks."

Rewards are different from incentives. Rewards are given after the behavior with the intention of improving or maintaining good behavior. Typical rewards that often fail to increase good behavior are grades, various certificates of recognition or special honors.

Grades are given in school to let kids know how they did, with the intention of encouraging good performance. But as any teacher in elementary, middle or high school can tell you, grades to some are unimportant and they fail to motivate. That's when grades are just a reward with very little incentive. Any time we realize a reward doesn't encourage good behavior, we need to look for an effective incentive to do the job.

Not only do rewards fail at times to encourage good behavior, they may even become a form of punishment. I've seen children who, because of their good grades, were selected to deliver an acceptance speech for some sort of honor, perhaps having the highest grades in school. So their "reward" is to deliver a speech, often for the first time, in front of several hundred strangers. For some kids that may in fact be punishment. How would you like that as a reward for good grades?

Haven't you known students who did so well in a subject that they were placed in honors classes as a reward? Usually those honor classes were far more difficult than the class in which the student did well. As an honor student he may actually make a lower grade than he would have in a regular class because the material is more difficult. Some "honor!"

When you want to reinforce a behavior, consider: "Is the reward I'm offering likely to increase the behavior I want? Will this really motivate this child to continue?" If yes, then you have an "incentive."

Words Make a Difference. Parents can use positive statements to gain a child's cooperation. For example:

- [ ] Now you've got it!
- [ ] You catch on fast!
- [ ] The best ever!
- [ ] You've made great use of your ability!
- [ ] I appreciate your helpfulness!
- [ ] It's great living with a kid like you!
- [ ] You're on the right track!
- [ ] I believe you've got it—super!
- [ ] Thanks for trying hard.
- [ ] You really stick to your work!
- [ ] Excellent!
- [ ] You're doing much better!
- [ ] That's your best ever!
- [ ] You did a first-rate job!
- [ ] What a dazzling job!

- [ ] You're helpfulness is appreciated.
- [ ] Way to go!
- [ ] Aren't you proud of the way you've improved?
- [ ] You're getting better every day!
- [ ] I am really pleased with your behavior!
- [ ] Isn't it nice to have the job done?
- [ ] I am proud of you!
- [ ] First-rate!
- [ ] Top-notch!
- [ ] I like living with you.
- [ ] Wow, you certainly used your time wisely!
- [ ] You really planned well!
- [ ] Fantastic!
- [ ] Your cooperation is helpful.
- [ ] You don't need anyone supervising you now!
- [ ] I feel good about your improvement.

Children warm to such statements and find them reassuring. The reinforcing message is intentionally left general, given for no particular behavior. It's not because, "You're good in soccer or gymnastics," but, "Just because you're you." Kids rarely hear too much of this kind of affirmation from their parents.

An Audience Makes a Difference. Twice in the New Testament God spoke publicly about his son, once at Jesus' baptism and again at his transfiguration. Here's what God said after Jesus was baptized, "This is my Son, whom I love; with him I am well pleased" (Matt. 3:17). God repeated that affirmation at the transfiguration, adding "Listen to him!" (Matt. 17:5).

How many times have you heard a parent say in front of friends or strangers, "This is my wonderful son. I'm very proud of him"? What do people hear you say about your child?

REVIEWING THE BASICS

What is discipline? It is helping kids to get their lives together. It is helping searchers find their destiny. It is teaching our children how to make responsible choices in life. It is using our own commmon sense.

Discipline is actually the most effective way of communicating our love as parents. We communicate love through real life experiences, modeling and opportunities to discover. We also communicate by questioning, reflecting, punishment and incentives.

Helping children make appropriate decisions takes them step by step closer to becoming responsible adults. Remember, it is the goal of Common Sense Discipline to help parents raise resourceful children who begin early making their own decisions.

2

Putting the Basics
to the Test

My first experience with a disobedient, rebellious and underachieving child was personal. I was one. My parents were good, God-fearing people who attended church regularly and provided well for my brother and me. They didn't deserve the hassles I gave them. While still in grade school I had to appear in juvenile court. Although my junior high years were uneventful, high school was miserable.

On the last day of classes my senior year of high school, we were sitting in Mr. Houchins' chemistry class. About five minutes left before the bell, Mr. Houchins suddenly turned and said to me, "Roger, you had a little help in this class, didn't you?" Suddenly it got very quiet as everyone turned to hear my answer.

"Uh, sure, Mr. Houchins," I stammered. "If you hadn't helped me with my homework and all, I never would have made it."

"No, that's not what I had in mind," he said. "See, when we had tests in here yours would often be turned in with seven or eight answers blank. Then when I passed the tests back out to be graded, yours would come back in with most of the right answers filled in. You had a little help in here, didn't you?"

At that very moment the bell rang, and I walked out devastated. I was in shock. It was probably the most humiliating experience of my life, and I well deserved it. For certain, Mr. Houchins would fail me. Ironically, I had already been accepted for college based on my advance entrance scores, assuming I graduated from high school. In order to graduate I needed one unit of science, and Mr. Houchins' chemistry class was it. So, besides the disgrace of being caught cheating, it appeared I wouldn't be going to college in the fall. After all of those years of hassling teachers and cheating, the chickens came home to roost.

My friends tried to cheer me up by saying, "C'mon, you know Houchins was only kidding. He wouldn't really fail you," except we knew I didn't have a chance.

"Are you kidding? You saw the look on his face." Failing would serve me right, and the way Mr. Houchins handled the entire matter had a ring of poetic justice to it.

Graduation was only two days away. Any minute I was expecting the phone to ring and for Mr. Houchins to tell my parents the bad news. But the call never came. After 24 hours my friends encouraged me again by saying, "Look, if Houchins was going to flunk you he would have called by now or sent your parents an official letter so they wouldn't show up for graduation and be embarrassed. He must have passed you." I began to breathe a little easier.

Finally, graduation night came. Everyone lined up in the State Fair Music Hall, since that was the only place in town large enough to accommodate our graduating class. All of the grandparents, aunts and uncles came for the occasion. The orchestra was playing "Pomp and Circumstance" and "Land of Hope and Glory" and all of the rest of the required music for graduation ceremonies. I stood around, joking nervously, waiting to march down the aisle, when suddenly someone came up behind me and slapped my shoulder. I stooped to pick up the program I dropped and turned to see Houchins staring me in the eye. I felt my heart stop.

"Oh, no," my mind began to race. "Here he's waited 'til the very last minute to tell me I flunked. There's no diploma down there with my name on it, and he's come to pull me out of line, saying I can't graduate." All my episodes of cheating flashed through my mind.

Then Houchins offered his hand to me and said, "Put 'er there, Roger. You'll do all right."

Relieved, all I could say was, "Thank you, Mr. Houchins. Thank you very much." And then he was gone.

For years I wondered how my life would have turned out had Mr. Houchins let me fail. I deserved it. Would I have gone on to college? What would my life be like today had Mr. Houchins not shown me mercy? I related this story to a colleague several years ago, and his response was, "Well, you probably would have gone to summer school and then entered college anyway. And if any other teachers had failed you earlier, you probably would have gotten your act together even sooner." Maybe, but I'm not sure.

For sure, I do know that Mr. Houchins' way of holding me responsible, while offering mercy, made a permanent difference in my life. Several years after graduation I wrote Mr. Houchins to let him know how things had gone since that night, to let him know that I've tried to do something worthwhile with my life. I don't know if he ever got the letter, but I wanted him to know that through nine years of college and three degrees, every grade I received, I earned. Mr. Houchins changed my life for the better because he believed in me. *Thanks, Mr. Houchins. I've tried to honor the chance you gave me.*

Yes, parents and teachers like Mr. Houchins often get a bum rap. They put up with lots they don't deserve. They hear about their failures but few of their successes. But keep trying, keep caring because working with children is the most important job you'll ever do. The little ways you give may change a life. It pays to look for ways to give special attention to each child.

WHY DO THEY ACT THAT WAY?

Rudolph Dreikurs, an expert in child psychology and classroom discipline, has identified four goals children often seek by their misbehavior. The following chart can be helpful to you in responding when your child misbehaves.

Why Do They Do That?			
Child's Actions	Parent's/ Teacher's Reaction	The Child's Goal	Options For Parents/Teachers
Nuisance Clown Lazy	**Irritated** Constant reminding and occasional yelling	**Attention** (Negative attention)	• Avoid giving negative attention. • Catch 'em being good • Affirm the child • **Use time-out for punishment**
Stubborn Argues Tells lies Disobedient	**Angry** Feels provoked and threatened	**Taking control** (Trying to lead)	• Refuse to argue • Let the child know that "he may be right" • Talk (later) about what's happening. • **Use negative practice for punishment**
Vicious Revengeful Lashes out	**Hurt** Tendency to retaliate	**Retaliation** (Payment for past hurt)	• Look for ways to encourage • Avoid the hurt reaction • **Use consequences for punishment**
Hopeless Helpless Gives up Loner	**Give up** Nothing seems to work	**Keep from trying** (If I don't try, I can't fail)	• Encourage efforts, not performance • Use reinforcement and incentives • Stop all criticism • **Focus on strengths**

Adapted from: *Discipline Without Tears*, Rudolf Dreikurs and Pearl Cassel.

If we think a child is continually acting up "just to get your goat," he is probably trying to do just that. If we "jump on his case," then we probably reinforce that child's misbehavior by our response. Any attention the child gets for acting up may simply encourage more misbehavior. It is important to get in touch with our reactions and feelings. They give a clue to what kind of attention our child is seeking. For instance, when you feel resentful and angry and you begin to question your love for this kid, then your child has probably been feeling anger and hostility toward you or somebody else.

THE DESPERATE KID'S NEGATIVE ATTENTION

It's a vicious cycle. The child acts up to get negative attention, we scold and punish the child, so he's reinforced by getting the negative attention, and the misbehavior intensifies. Then we try avoiding the child because he's so obnoxious. The parent feels guilty. The child, feeling ignored and unwanted, seeks more attention. By this time he may have *forgotten* how to get positive attention or may have decided that negative attention is easier to get, so he simply does the same thing he did before and acts up again. And the cycle goes round and round.

Attention to a child is like water to a thirsty person. Really desperate kids will do almost anything to get that attention. If you were stranded in the desert without hope of rescue, you'd risk drinking polluted water just to stay alive.

Children who are desperate for attention will sometimes do desperate things to get attention. It may "work" for a while, but it always makes things worse. Negative attention doesn't satisfy like positive attention. When children are quite small they naturally get lots of attention just for being babies, all cute and cuddly. After awhile many kids stop getting as much attention as they'd like, so they just continue acting like a baby.

If children aren't getting enough positive attention, they'll get attention of one sort or another, one way or the other. That's why many kids seem to act up on purpose even when it's obvious they're about to be punished.

NEGATIVE ATTENTION IS BETTER THAN NONE

Children who are continually ignored by a parent can become emotionally neglected and severely depressed. At times their need for attention may be so great that they will deliberately goad the neglectful parent to the point of child abuse. They know that after the abuse takes place, the parent's next actions will usually be some sort of attention, if only out of guilt. While that may sound extreme to you, I have observed it in some of the families I have seen, and the same pattern has been verified by colleagues.

In a similar fashion it's not uncommon for some teenage girls to become sexually involved with boys as a substitute for the normal attention and affection they should be receiving from their fathers. Unfortunately, things often get out of control and some of these girls wind up pregnant. That's one sure way to finally get Dad's attention, but the price is far too high.

If your child has been acting up and you suspect he's trying to get negative attention, before responding with the typical lecture or unnecessary spanking, talk openly about what you've seen and share how you feel about the situation. One father said it like this: "If you want my attention, that isn't the way to go about getting it. What you're doing just gets me angry. Now do you want something?" His child said "yes" and then Dad stated, "I'll be glad to give you some attention if you'll tell me just what you want to do." It helps to talk about the situation with the child. The key for parents is to be perceptive. Look for the message behind the behavior. Use this open discussion to help the child change his pattern and break the habit.

COMMON SENSE DISCIPLINE AT SCHOOL

In the Classroom

Frequently at school-sponsored in-service workshops for teachers I hear, "Roger, I've got this kid in my class who acts like a brat unless I make him move his chair next to my desk. Then he's fine so long as I keep a close watch over him. After a week, when you'd think he's had enough of that, I let him move back to sit with the rest of the students and soon he's acting like a brat all over again. What do you suggest?"

"If I act like a brat can I sit real close to you, too?" You see, without intending to, you may be reinforcing the very behavior you want to eliminate by the attention you give it. Let's face it, when he sits next to you, the obnoxious kid gets to see all the grades the other kids get as you put them in the grade book, he gets to hear every message other teachers give you and he gets to see everyone who walks by the door. Besides that, he's at the front of the room where he can make faces at all the other students. It's like putting a clown at center stage. Some punishment for a clown!

It might be necessary to move the student to the back of the room where he has as little attention as possible, since that's what seems to reinforce him.

Here's another way punishment can be rewarding in school: Suppose a student, for one reason or another, can't stand to be in a particular class. Maybe it's the subject matter, a personality clash with the teacher, problems with other students or all three. Because this student resents being in that class he begins to misbehave. As a result of his deliberate goading, his teacher becomes livid (in case of personality clash, this is reinforcing enough for many students as a "get back"), until she finally gives up on him and sends him to the principal's office for punishment. But the problem is that he wanted out of that very class to begin with, so his teacher has just reinforced him for his negative behavior. It's like the police giving movie tickets when they stop someone for speeding.

In the School Office

When some students are sent to the office, several useless messages may be conveyed to the student: 1) the teacher doesn't know what to do with you; 2) the teacher is passing the buck to someone else, or 3) if you are bad enough in this class, you don't have to do your work for the day.

If that's not enough to get you to stop sending students to the office, then think about the reward factor. Going to the office is fascinating. Think about it—you get to hear who calls in sick, who's tardy, who's new, and almost every teacher who comes in will stop and ask, "What are you doing here?" You'll get to tell your tale of misbehavior over and over. About the worst punishment you'll get is a couple of licks. For some kids that's a cheap price to pay for all the attention they are bound to get, on top of not having to remain in a class they wanted out of in the first place. Some punishment!

COMMON SENSE THAT WORKS

In-School Suspension

Instead of sending an uncooperative student to the office, a few periods of In-School Suspension (ISS) may be useful. An In-School Suspension system is a positive alternative to ordinary suspension or expulsion. When you think about it, it doesn't make much sense to allow a student who doesn't want to cooperate with school in the first place the privilege of not going to school because he didn't act right.

In-School Suspension is for those students who have consistently refused to cooperate with school rules and who have been uncooperative in class. When they refuse to cooperate, they are sent to an ISS room which ideally has few desks, few windows, if any, is boring to be in and where cooperation is mandatory. The teacher or monitor in charge needs to be an old hand at teaching, one not easily fooled by manipulative students and who accepts no nonsense from disobedient students.

Initial ISS time may be for several periods from the same class. For example, "George, you will now have to go to ISS for third period for the next three days because Mrs. Jones referred you for lack of cooperation." There is no negotiation accepted from the student at this point. The referring teacher's word is final. She sends the ISS monitor a set of activities for George to complete before he's allowed to return to his regular class. In no case is George allowed to return to class early, no matter how well he does his work or how fast. If he completes the assignments for ISS early, then the monitor requests additional work from the referring teacher, or she may give George other problems to work on.

Another initial ISS period may be for one to three class days in which the student spends the entire day, including lunch, in ISS isolated from other students. The only exceptions to this are *very short* breaks, perhaps once in the morning and once after lunch, to go to the rest room. Complete quiet and good behavior is expected. ISS is similar to Detention Hall, with the exception that in ISS, students must complete assigned work or face additional ISS for continued lack of cooperation.

Obviously, being a monitor for ISS will not be a popular task. Perhaps an additional incentive can be offered those teachers who volunteer and who are qualified. One possibility might be having monitors serve for only one week at a time while an experienced substitute is paid for taking over their regular class. Other districts might have monitors serve only one day at a time, but I'd think the lack of continuity while a student works off ISS time would not be helpful.

Occasionally you might have a teacher who prefers ISS to regular teaching because theoretically there would be relatively few students to deal with and then only for a few days at a time.

If you're serious about starting an ISS program at your school, check with other districts and see how they handle suspensions. You might contact the staff of an education department at a good teachers' college and see what they recommend. Remember, ISS is for schools that are serious about offering a useful alternative to expulsion for problem students. After only a few periods in ISS most students will be more than willing to return to their regular classes and cooperate. But if they haven't decided to cooperate after an initial ISS referral, send them to ISS again, for a longer period this time.

What You Say Is What You Get

As you learn how children get negative attention, you can begin to look for better ways to reinforce them. At first, with some children, you may have to look long and hard to find something good to say. But even the most obnoxious kid has his moments when he forgets to misbehave and may lapse into a neutral state. That's when you need to seize the moment and say something nice like, "I sure have enjoyed the way you've been watching TV quietly these past few minutes." A typical conniving child, upon hearing you say something like this, will stare at you with an incredulous look, as if thinking, "What? Me acting good? Just what do you have up your sleeve? Are you fixing to pull something on me?"

Don't pour it on too thick at first. Avoid the temptation to add, "You were sure obnoxious earlier. It's good to see you acting nice now." He may have been obnoxious earlier, but reminding him of it after he's changed for the better just muddies the water.

Some time ago I was visiting friends whose children I had never met. As I drove up, out came George and Gracie's two sons, ages three and six. When I got out of the car George's oldest son introduced himself and said, "Hi, I'm Billy and this is my brother, Bobby. He's shy." Bobby, who had been smiling until that remark, promptly hung his head.

"Hi, Bobby. How are you?" No response from Bobby.

About that time George came out and said, "Hi, Roger, have you met the kids? This is our oldest, Billy, and here's Bobby; he's the shy one."

We all walked inside and George's father greeted me with, "Roger, how good to see you again. Have you met everyone? Here's Billy and there's Bobby. He's shy."

"Incredible," I thought. "I've been here less than five minutes and already three generations of Bobby's family have told me he's shy."

"Wherever you are, Bobby, my hat's off to you, pal. You are a neat little guy, but you're gonna need lots of other voices to counteract those three. I doubt you started off feeling shy, but it's easy to see what keeps you feeling that way."

Negative Commands

Just as important as *what* we say to a child is *how* we say it. Have you ever made plans with another parent to go out for the evening while the children were left with a sitter? As you were leaving your friend's house, perhaps she said something like this to her kids: "Now while we're gone don't give the baby-sitter a bad time, no pillow fights or mess-making in the kitchen. And don't stay up late watching the late movie." The problem with such statements is their potential to backfire on the parent.

Her children imagined the message like this: "Yea! We haven't had a baby-sitter that we could hassle in a long time, so tonight's our chance! Let's have a pillow fight just as soon as Mom is out the door. Then we'll fix some really good stuff in the kitchen and eat anywhere we want. We can make popcorn and stay up late for the midnight movie. Wow, what a night it's going to be!"

Poor baby-sitter, she has my sympathy. Mom's statements, "Don't do—," are called negative commands in the communications business. To understand any negative command a child must first imagine *doing* the very thing we want him to *avoid*. It's as if I say, "Whatever you do for the next 15 minutes, don't think about a white elephant."

"White elephants? I haven't thought of a white elephant in ages, but now that you've brought the subject up, that's all I can think about." That's exactly what negative commands do, make us think about the very thing we wanted to avoid in the first place.

Several years ago we were driving from Texas to the southeast to visit relatives. As we began to cross the Mississippi River bridge on Interstate 10 at Baton Rouge, I noticed a sign put up by the highway department that said, "Don't look at boats." Naturally the first thing I thought about was all the boats that were bound to be on the mighty Mississippi. So I glanced over to look, just like any other visitor who had been reminded of the boats. Apparently so many other drivers looked too that the highway department erected a solid fence along the bridge rail to block the view their sign had just called to our attention.

POSITIVE DIRECTIONS

I wonder what would have happened to drivers on the bridge if the sign simply read, "Watch cars for sudden stops!" Now that probably would have kept my attention on my driving. By the way, you're still not thinking about white elephants, are you?

Teachers sometimes inadvertently use negative commands by saying, "Class, I'm going to the office for about ten minutes. While I'm gone I want no cheating, no talking and no getting out of your chairs." What the students imagined was something like, "While the teacher's gone, you'll have about nine minutes to copy from your neighbor's paper, or you can talk and walk around the room but better be back at your desks in ten minutes because that's how long it takes to walk to the office and back."

A much better way for the teacher to state this message would be, "Class, I'm stepping outside the door briefly. Continue to do your work quietly and remain at your desks. Those students who are doing what I asked when I return will receive five bonus points."

TIME FOR THE TEST

Understanding why children do what they do helps parents and teachers select the most appropriate method of discipline for any given situation. And, this is the place to start.

Common Sense Discipline can work in even the toughest of school systems. If these principles work in schools, then they can work in your home.

It's time to put Common Sense Discipline to the test.

3

Discipline That Makes A Difference

"**R**oger, nothing seems to work with this kid of mine. I've tried everything—spanking, grounding, sending him to his room. I feel like a failure. I think it's hopeless." Can you identify with that? I hear it in my office frequently.

About a year ago I got a sore throat and started looking in the medicine cabinet for something to take. After searching I found some pills left from a previous trip to the doctor for the same problem, so I took those for three days and felt much better. Three days later the sore throat came right back, worse this time, so I called the doctor's office. When I told his nurse what had happened and what medication I had taken, she started laughing. Her laughter embarrassed me; I've never been altogether comfortable being laughed at. This time I learned firsthand that you have to take the right medication, and it takes a full seven days to do the trick.

I'm convinced now those stick-on labels that say, "Take all of this medication until empty unless otherwise directed by your physician," were directed at me.

Discipline works a lot like medicine.Sometimes you have to keep giving it until the job is done. Many different kinds of discipline work fine if you will use them long enough. Too many parents stop using good discipline measures before they can take effect.

This chapter describes discipline techniques. Let me describe four common sense techniques that can be readily adapted to each child or situation. In fact, God uses these same methods in disciplining his children. All four methods can be used effectively during the first 11 or so years. The first two methods are more appropriate for teen years (11-18). Here are the methods:

1. Catch 'em doing something right
2. Logical consequences
3. Time-out
4. Negative practice

CATCH 'EM DOING SOMETHING RIGHT

It takes time to make any kind of discipline work. It's the kind of love God showed his son when he said, "This is my beloved son." It's the kind of discipline God showed the children of Israel as he led them out of Egypt and reminded them of his presence in a pillar of cloud by day and fire by night (Exodus 13:21) and when he fed them manna (Exodus 16).

The Power of a Positive Word

These days most of the reminders kids hear focus on their problems. Kids hear about their mistakes from everyone. Think how much better off children would be if they heard positive reminders that regardless of their failures, they are moving in the right direction.

The meanest kid I ever knew was William. He was twelve years old, and his home was like a combat zone. His parents had lots of problems, and William had absorbed many of them. Placed in a camp for disturbed children where Kathy and I were counselors, William sought to test and break every rule he could. At first he did a pretty good job of it. I said he was mean; he was also obnoxious, as obnoxious as they come.

On one particularly rough day with William, it struck me that about 90% of the attention he received from adults was for his misbehavior. Yet even at his worse he was only ornery about 10% of the time. The rest of the time he was either neutral or acceptable. Yet the bulk of his attention from adults focused on the small percentage of his misbehavior. Talk about negative attention!

So Kathy and I started looking for positive things to say about William. At first we had to look long and hard, but you usually find what you look for, and so did we. We started telling William when he was doing OK and some of the things we liked about him. We didn't unload all at once because, after all, we didn't want him to get whiplash. The more we talked about positives, the more there were to talk about. Slowly, like a huge ship turning, William started coming around.

Start Right Now

What would happen if right now you put this book down and caught your children doing something right? What would they do if you told them how pleased you were? Would they pass out from shock and surprise? Why don't you try it? Take a chance! If they're small, they'll probably eat it up. If they're teenagers, they'll probably act embarrassed. Don't make a big deal of it, just something like, "I appreciate the way you put forth an effort." Or, "I know school is tough right now with all the pressures, and I want you to know that I care about you." Who knows? If it worked for William, it can work for you, too.

Speaking up about the good things shows you're thinking about the good that's present in all children. It's accentuating the positive. When was the last time you surprised your children with an "I love you" statement? Do you like to hear that? What would happen if you started to sprinkle a few compliments here and there? You'll never know for sure until you try.

LOGICAL CONSEQUENCES

Dr. Rudolph Dreikurs is usually associated with popularizing the concept of logical consequences with children. In scripture logical consequences are described by God throughout Exodus 21-23. There God outlines a number of rules and the consequences for breaking them. If the rule was broken accidentally (Exodus 22:5), then repayment was based on an equal basis. If a deliberate theft took place, repayment might range from four to five times the value of what was stolen (Exodus 22:1).

The term "logical consequence" derives its name from a logical relationship between what is expected *and* what takes place. Think of it as an "if/then" relationship. "*If* you don't, *then* you won't."

Consequences Speak Louder

The value of logical consequences comes from permitting children to experience the results or consequences of their actions. For example, "If you continue to play with your milk, then it may spill. That will be all the milk you'll get for this meal." For logical consequences to work the parents must be willing to allow children to experience some unpleasant consequences, like doing without more milk, if the kids are to learn how life really works. Allowing Lane to walk around the fountain was an example of logical consequences (chapter 1). Certainly you should never permit your child to risk any physical danger just to teach a lesson, but allowing an occasional bump or unpleasant experience will often teach far more than warnings or lectures.

Logical consequences can also have a positive result. For example, "If you continue to work hard, then you can expect to be given more hours and maybe more responsibility." Or, "If you continue to save your allowance, then you'll soon have enough to buy the game you've been wanting."

Dr. David Premack suggested two general logical consequences that are known as the grandparents' rules:

Grandma's Rule: "No ice cream until you eat your vegetables," or "You get to do what you want after you do what I want you to do."

Grandpa's Rule: "If you break it, then you fix it," or "If you make a mess, then you have to clean it up."

Roger's Rule: "If you want something extra, then you will have to figure out how to earn it," or "When your allowance is used up you'll have to find ways to make extra money."

Natural Consequences

Sometimes logical consequences occur naturally, without parents having to do anything out of the ordinary. For example, "If you leave your textbook outside, the rain may ruin it, and you'll be responsible for buying a new one." Most logical consequences are set up by parents using "if/ then" wording which permits children to learn by experience.

You may have noticed that most children try to manipulate parents when first presented with logical consequences, "Oh, Mom, please, can't you wait just 15 minutes longer?" If you let your child manipulate you, then logical consequences won't work. If you let your children experience some disappointment as a result of their misbehavior they'll take you seriously next time. Many parents could save themselves a lot of anguish at mealtimes by simply telling children when dinner is ready and then sit down and eat when it's served. Or they may call children in once and only once from playing, and then sit down to eat. If Junior comes in on time, then he'll have a hot meal with the rest of the family. If he doesn't, then he won't. I know it sounds harsh, but, believe me, it is not. It's teaching about life. How many parents do you know who call their children again and again, "Come in now, I said!"

Schedules and Promptness

Many things in our lives operate by the standards of logical consequences. If we intend for our children to become competent in dealing with the workaday world, then it's vital for them to learn how to deal with the consequences. Schedules and promptness depend on logical consequences. So, "If you are ready when the school bus comes, then you'll get to ride it to school. If you aren't ready on time, then you'll probably miss the bus and be tardy." How many of you have remembered late Saturday afternoon that what you wanted to wear to church the next day was in the cleaners? Then you rushed to the cleaners only to arrive five minutes after they closed for the weekend. That's how it works in real life.

Fines and Penalties

Have you ever thought about how many fines and penalties there are in life? Overdue library books, late payment fees, cars parked at a meter too long and traffic violations are all subject to fines. At home and in school fines can be applied in the form of detentions, extra work and even money. One mother with four children had a nightmare each time she took them shopping. "I want this," and "Buy me that." You know the routine. Invariably Mom would wind up spending a small fortune on food for bribes just to shut the kids up, which only reinforced them to beg and holler next time.

I suggested she begin the next shopping trip by announcing, "Today we're going shopping. I'm going to give each of you enough money to buy one ice cream cone (she had been spending more than that, anyway). If you act up, argue or fight, I'll fine you five cents for each time, and you'll have to pay me right then out of your ice cream money (she kept the two youngest kids' money to avoid their losing it). When we get to the ice cream parlor at the end of our shopping (arranged that way on purpose), you can buy anything you want with your money or you can save it for another time."

The logical consequence at the end of their shopping was that those who had behaved could still afford an ice cream cone and those who had acted up went without. Her kids improved dramatically in just one trip using this consequence. (Some kids need more than one time.) Mom began to enjoy shopping for the first time in years. Eventually the kids acted right, without needing the ice cream money, because good behavior became a habit.

TIME-OUT

Time-out is a little like "go stand in the corner" for a specified amount of time. However, there's more to it than that. Time-out is removing your child from the present situation and giving him some time to think. God used the wilderness as a perfect time-out place for his children when they misbehaved. The desert was a great place to think —there was little else to do for forty years.

For a pre-school child I use three minutes for the first time-out of the day, and for a school-aged child I begin with five minutes. If your child needs a second time-out later that day for the *same behavior*, start with 6 minutes and then 9 minutes for the third time-out. I recommend you start at the beginning for a different misbehavior and always start each day with a clean slate.

An ideal time-out corner has no windows to look out and nothing handy to play with. Preferably it's a boring spot away from the main activity in your house. You should be able to see your child at all times, but he must face away from you into the corner. If you don't have any corners handy, you might tell your child to face the wall halfway down a hallway, sit on the edge of the bathtub or stand in a utility room so long as the door remains open and you can see him easily. Friends, brothers and sisters aren't allowed to talk to a child in time-out or else they get a time-out of their own.

Getting Started Right

For safety's sake and to avoid panic, *never* put a child in a small confined place like a closet and *never* close the door of the room when a child is in time-out. When you first begin using time-out, periodically check on your child to see how he's doing. Avoid using time-out for children who are prone to daydream, since time-out will be a rewarding place to daydream more. Depressed children will only become more depressed in time-out, so try something different, perhaps negative practice (more on that later).

Time-out is suitable for misbehavior like refusing to cooperate, deliberately moving slowly (stalling for time), or doing something other than what you told your child to do like continuing to watch TV after you said, "Turn it off." When Lane needs time-out Kathy or I will say, "All right, Lane, that's time-out because you kept on . . . . Go to the time-out corner and stay there until the timer goes off." Then we set the timer on our kitchen stove.

If you need to buy a timer there are small digital models that can be easily programmed for 1-100 minutes and are magnetized to stay on your refrigerator. Punch in the time you want, like a calculator, press "start," and go about your business.

If your child starts to yell or ask, "How much longer?" answer, "Each time you yell or leave the corner I'll add one more minute to your time. Stay there quietly until the timer goes off." If he continues to complain keep adding extra minutes up to a maximum of ten beyond the original time. This works for most kids, but if yours tests you beyond the extra ten minutes you'll need to shift gears and try something different.

Time-out for Small Children

Small children can be put in time-out by using a high chair with the seat and crotch belts safely fastened so your child can't climb or slip out. Adjust the tray snugly up so your child is better restrained and can't loosen the safety belts. Place the high chair far enough away from the wall so he can't push himself over backwards with his feet and can't reach or grab anything. It will work best if your child can't see or hear you easily. We started putting Lane in time-out when he was 14 months old when he seemed to take great delight in filling his hands with food and smearing the stuff all over his high chair. Time-out worked! He stopped!

Some parents use a playpen for time-out. Just be sure there are no toys to play with and that the mesh is small enough to keep buttons and snaps on your child's clothing from getting caught. At first most small children will cry and scream like a stuck pig when placed in time-out. It usually takes them five to ten times in time-out before they'll settle down and get quiet quickly. It takes that long for them to learn that the time-out period is short and that when the timer goes off they'll be able to return to their play. It's important for you to do your part by letting a child out of time-out as soon as the timer goes off.

Children who are too old for a high chair or playpen can be told to sit in a small chair which will reduce the temptation for them to walk off. If they won't stay in the chair, then strap them in with a belt. By age three or four most children will cooperate by sitting in the chair. By age eight most can stand facing the wall.

Occasionally a small child will *not* leave time-out even when the timer has sounded and his parents have given permission to leave. The child's embarrassment and shame keep him there, and he may be trying to put a little guilt on you for putting him in time-out. If this happens just say, "You are welcome to leave time-out as soon as you decide, but if you want to stay, that's up to you. When you feel like getting out of time-out and having fun again, you may." Then the parent should leave the room to avoid giving the child negative attention for having stayed in time-out too long.

The Place for Time-out

Most children's rooms are so full of toys, electronic gear and books that sending a child to his room is not the place for time-out. Besides, do you want to associate the place where your child sleeps and plays with punishment?

Some parents will send their child out of a room, "Until you can behave." When that happens the child usually walks halfway down the hall, realizes he's about to miss out on the best part of the TV show, and suddenly decides to be good. This is actually a form of manipulation because the child simply cooperates with time-out until he's ready to switch it off on his own terms. It doesn't work that way in real life. In real life, once the blinking red lights appear in the rear view mirror, you're going to get a ticket. It doesn't matter how nice you are between the time you get the ticket and when you pay it, the fine is still the same. And if you get too sassy with the officer giving you the ticket, something else may be added to it as well.

Giving Instructions Once

Usually one warning is appropriate for each new problem, sometimes none if the child clearly knows his actions are off limits. Once the warning has been issued, be ready to follow through with an appropriate consequence. After all, each traffic signal has one caution light, but when the signal turns red, it's time to stop.

Many parents will count from one to three before following through with some consequence. I saw a funny example of this with some friends. They had two children, ages two and four. Betty, the four-year-old, was playing in the back yard. Dad came out and said, "Betty, it's time for supper." Betty kept right on playing, acting as if she hadn't heard, even though it was obvious she had. "Betty," he said, "come in right now!" You know the routine. Betty went right on playing and jumping around, dah-te-dah-te-dah. "Betty! That's ONE!" dah-te-dah-te-dah. "That's TWO!" Same song and dance from Betty. "That's TWO AND ONE-HALF—, TWO AND THREE-FOURTHS—TWO AND SEVEN-EIGHTS, ALL RIGHT! THAT DOES IT. DO I HAVE TO GET MY BELT?" It wasn't until Dad's voice got loud enough and his look stern enough that Betty decided she had waited as long as she dared. Then she came in. Her only punishment was Dad's loud voice.

Actually, I was impressed. After all, here was this four-year-old who ordinarily wouldn't learn fractions until the third grade and already her father was teaching them. Imagine that! He actually said, "Two and seven-eights!" Betty knew Dad well enough to stall until his breaking point was almost reached. I wonder what would have happened if Dad simply had told her once that supper was ready and then had gone back inside to eat.

NEGATIVE PRACTICE

Negative practice combines time-out with children *practicing* the very action you want them to stop, over and over for three to five minutes. It works because most children soon get tired of misbehaviors they are told they *have* to do. Remember the goal is to help the child. For example, "Because you kept jumping on the bed after I told you to stop, go over to the time-out corner and jump up and down until the timer goes off." As with regular time-out, walk away as soon as you set the timer or else your child will try to talk you out of the punishment or will ask you endless questions to diminish the boredom. Be sure the timer is well out of his reach, preferably in another room, where he can still hear it go off. Periodically check to be sure your child is cooperating with your instructions.

Negative practice makes misbehaviors boomerang and then stop due to saturation. Once most of us become saturated with an activity, we soon tire of it. Many of the negative things kids do to get attention are appealing because they know it's against the rules. Giving children "permission" to repeat those things in a time-out corner for three to five minutes soon spoils the taboo appeal.

If you have a stubborn child who likes to test your resolve, he might say, "I'll stay in the corner, but you can't make me jump up and down." I would say, "Of course not and I wouldn't think of trying to make you, but for every minute you stall me by not jumping, you're going to lose three minutes from your next TV show or play activity, and you have just lost three minutes for stalling. As soon as you decide to start jumping up and down, tell me so I'll know when to stop counting your penalty time." Then walk out of the room. If your child remains in time-out until the timer goes off, but never begins to jump, no problem. It'll just catch up with him later when he wants to start watching TV or play outside. Simply say, "Ordinarily that would be fine with me, but remember earlier when I told you to jump up and down and you refused to do it? That was 30 minutes ago and three times 30 is 90 minutes or one and one-half hours. That's how long you're going to have to wait before watching TV or going outside to play. If bedtime comes before you use up the time, you'll just have to finish the remaining penalty tomorrow."

PARENTS SHOULD TEST THE KIDS

I believe that parents should always have the ultimate say, but at times all kids need enough rope to hang themselves, so to speak. Remember, God led his children of Israel into the desert, gave them instructions and rules. He tested them to see what was in their hearts — to see how mature they were. Parents have to test, too. The kid might think he's getting away with something but remember, he still has to face the music later. Keep track of how long he stalled. Later, when he finally decides to cooperate, his penalty would be that amount of time, either in time-out or by being restricted to the house. I would customize the penalty to fit the circumstances best.

Key to Success

A little punishment often works better than a lot. That's why no TV for 5 minutes is often worse than no TV for the evening. Restrict a child from TV for the evening, and he'll simply find something else to do for fun. Make him miss 5 minutes while standing in time-out, and he's dying to get back and see what he's missing. Forget grounding for a month or longer because it will punish the whole family as much as the child. A little discipline carefully designed is better than a lot.

This One Is Hopeless

Occasionally a parent asks my advice for help with a child who is completely out of control. In such cases I would consider spanking small children. If the child continues to test me some more, I'd spank again. For older children and teenagers I'd consider stripping their rooms bare of nonessential clothes and furniture, leaving them with the basics only: a bed, desk, chest of drawers and the necessary clothes in their closets. Then anything they wanted back they'd have to earn back. I'd make out a list of the "prices" of things and what it would take to get them back in terms of hours of study, improved grades, work around the house and so on. I wouldn't make it unreasonable or hopeless to obtain but sufficiently serious to show that I meant business.

This worked well with one especially sullen and sassy teenager. It took one week for her to realize her parents were no longer going to put up with her disobedience. Some children are almost daring their parents to lay down the law. When that happens, you'll be doing your kids a favor if you do. When the kids are honest they'll tell you they want to be disciplined.

CONSIDERING THE OPTIONS

We've now overviewed the four methods of Common Sense Discipline. The methods are Catch'Em Doing Something Right, Logical Consequences, Time-out and Negative Practice. Each of these methods can be adapted to each child and any situations.

The rest of this book will show you how these methods work in actual practice at each age level. Remember to emphasize the positive. Mention the things you appreciate and notice what they do well, like: "I really appreciate the pleasant way you've been acting this morning. It's fun to be with you." Positive statements from you will help all the discipline methods work better.

Remember the goal: Common Sense Discipline can help you raise resourceful children who have learned how to be responsible adults.

4

Guiding Their First Steps

12-30 Months

Of all the lessons you want your child to learn, which is most important during the early years? Obeying, walking, talking or sharing? What's the most important thing you want to teach your child during this period?

When Lane was this age, more than anything else I wanted him to learn about love. Love is, without a doubt, the foundation of all those other lessons. My boy needed to learn about love from *his* parents.

THE NATURE OF LOVE

Real love is doing something for someone else that you don't have to do, that you *may not even want to do*, but that you *choose* to do because you have the other person's best interest at heart. Our attitude should be like Jesus':

> Who, being in very nature God, did not consider equality with God something to be grasped, but made himself nothing, taking the very nature of a servant, being made in human likeness. And being found in appearance as a man, he humbled

73

himself and became obedient to death—even death on a cross!

Philippians 2:6-8

Babies provide us with on-the-job love experience. Love becomes our choice even if it means changing dirty diapers, changing plans or changing our mind.

Since 1977 when I began using this example, I've only heard one adult say she actually enjoyed changing dirty diapers, and I think she may have been a bit disturbed. The fact of the matter is that changing dirty diapers is an unpleasant business, at least for the person doing the changing. Now I could enjoy getting up at 3:00 AM to comfort a frightened child because I love the feeling I have when my youngster feels reassured. But changing dirty diapers? It's a dirty, stinking job, that's for sure. We do it because we love. We do it even when we don't feel like it— because we love.

"Fathers, do you love your baby?" Simply because I did some everyday things for my son that I didn't always want to do, like changing diapers when he needed them changed and a host of other acts, my son gradually came to appreciate and then to love the attention he received from me. All along the journey of parenthood you will do some things that you don't want to do, things that you need to do because you love. When your child responds, you will feel the love. You both give and receive.

Chart 2 on the next page indicates the need for parents and teachers to make the major decisions for infants—that's common sense! There is, however, a need for little babies to be able to pick and choose very early in life. It's great practice for the big decisions later on.

FIRST SIX MONTHS

During the first six months of life, I believe the most important discipline your child needs is your love, atten-

Common Sense Discipline Chart 2

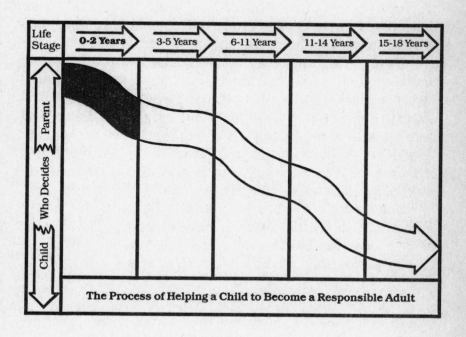

Life Stage	0-2 Years	3-5 Years	6-11 Years	11-14 Years	15-18 Years

The Process of Helping a Child to Become a Responsible Adult

tion and protection. Our pediatrician told us shortly after Lane was born that for the first six months, "You can't spoil him by giving too much attention." I'm telling you the same thing. During this time, talking, playing and protecting are the most important kinds of discipline to teach.

A child's life prior to this century was somewhat bleak. Even as late as the 19th Century it was the parent's job to be harsh, firm and restrictive. Only recently have we realized that children need comfort, help and encouragement. Dr. Lloyd deMause, an American psychohistorian and editor of *History of Childhood Quarterly*, has found that not only do children need help in growing up, but that feeling empathy toward children is a relatively new experience in American history.

God has helped us to begin to understand the tender nurture needed in childhood. And we are finding effective ways of encouraging the growth of our children. But parents of infants must also at times be "lovingly restrictive."

When your child starts to crawl is the time to start showing some restrictive discipline in the form of shielding electrical outlets, locking dangerous chemicals and cleaning supplies out of reach and sight, and keeping sharp and dangerous objects out of reach. An occasional, "No," followed by clapping your hands once and then moving your child if necessary, can be useful. Make it easy on both of you and recognize the obvious.

Small children will try to get into things, if only out of curiosity. Usually it's easier to move something to another shelf once, than continually to tell your child, "No." Make this as pleasant as possible for both of you.

SIX TO THIRTY MONTHS

During the first thirty months of your child's life there will be numerous opportunities for you to show acts of love. These first few years are full of exciting changes in you and your child. Have you thought about how *you* change during these months? The baby makes dramatic changes. You'll witness some important changes in your baby including: walking (12-18 months), talking (12-24 months), toilet training (18-30 months) and temper tantrums (18-30 months). Let's start with the fun part.

Walking

Some children crawl lots before they start walking; some just seem to get up one day and walk on their own. Walking is probably learned as a combination of instinct and imitation. For months your baby has noticed all of the fun things you keep up high and how he's enjoyed riding while you've been walking. When the time is right he'll try walking on his own.

When Your Child Is Hurt

Learning to walk is reinforced by praise and encouragement. It's also accompanied by falls and bumps. The way parents respond to these accidents will teach children a great deal about pain.

For most young children, pain is largely psychological. That's not to say children don't get hurt physically; they do. But a great deal of their pain can be avoided if parents respond appropriately to accidents. It's important for parents to help children minimize the effects of pain because so many bumps are inevitable during this period, and unnecessary attention for pain will teach children to become whiners and cry babies. Adult hypochondriacs don't get that way by accident.

Next time you're around a toddler and his parents, watch what happens when the toddler falls. Usually the child will immediately look to Mom and Dad for a reaction. If they say in alarm, "Oh, my poor darling, are you hurt? Are you all right?" you can expect Junior to get scared and start crying. Then Mom or Dad will pick him up and sympathize with him, which only reinforces Junior's decision to get scared and cry.

Asking a child, "Are you hurt?" is like my asking you, "Are you thinking of a white elephant again?" "Are you hurt?" guarantees that the child will think about pain. Our looks of alarm and concern will trigger Junior to get scared and cry, if for no other reason than our scared facial expressions.

When a child stumbles and falls parents might try saying, "OK?" with a questioning but reassuring expression.

Instead of showing shock and alarm, a matter-of-fact attitude says, "It's all right to have bumps and falls." If the child continues to stay on the floor, say, "Need a hand?" instead of, "Here, let me help you up," which would suggest he probably can't handle this problem.

Rather than give too much attention to pain, here are three caring statements to make when your child is definitely hurt:

1. "I know it hurts" acknowledges the pain and shows that you understand what your child is experiencing.
2. "It will get better" offers reassurance that the pain doesn't last forever.
3. "Tell me when you feel better" distracts your child from the pain and has a positive, self-fulfilling prophetic effect.

Using these three statements with Lane brought some pleasant results. One is that he has a very high tolerance to pain. He rarely cries in response to a bump or sickness, but when he does, we know that he's genuinely in pain. A lighter note occurred once when some friends were visiting, and their children were playing with Lane in his room. In his excitement, Lane fell and bruised his knee. In obvious pain, he came limping to me for comfort. After I used the three caring statements, Lane got up, still limping but eager to return to his friends, and said, "I feel better now, Daddy. I feel better." (I'm still not sure which one of us was reassuring the other.)

Baby-Proofing Your House

Most parents automatically "baby-proof" their houses by removing glass objects and padding sharp corners where possible. While it's a good idea to remove all the potentially dangerous objects infants may be attracted to, have you replaced those things with safe substitutes for your child to play with? Here's how we did it. In our living room there are two cabinets in the bottom of a bookcase. Lane could easily crawl into the cabinets and reach the first shelf above the cabinets. We could see that it was going to be trouble, trouble, trouble keeping him away from valuable objects, so we decided to store some of Lane's favorite toys there. We reserved the two cabinets and the first shelf for his friends and him.

When our friends came over with their children we'd open the cabinets and tell the kids, "Here are some things for you to play with," and the kids would make a beeline for them. Because the toys were in easy reach, all the children tended to stay in the immediate area around the cabinets. Occasionally a child would climb into the cabinets and close the doors, but that was all part of their fun. Having only toys in the cabinets and shelf made clean-up easy, too. We'd toss the toys into the cabinets and shut the doors. The most appealing toys went on the first shelf in plain view. When the kids came over again they'd go straight for the cabinets and take out the toys and begin playing. At first their parents would scold them for their assertiveness and for "Not asking first," but we'd reassure the parents, "It's okay; they know that's what the toys are there for."

Christmas Trees

Your child's first or second Christmas tree can be a special memory, or it can be a real headache depending on how you arrange things. Some parents unnecessarily spend time spanking a child's hands for touching the ornaments. That seems a bit naive and unrealistic because the ornaments are pretty to look at and fascinating to touch. Say "No" in such a situation and you set yourself up for defiance.

One unconventional couple decided to suspend their Christmas tree from the ceiling so that it was off the floor, above their toddler's reach. That way everyone could enjoy it without having to fuss at the child. Granted, it did look a bit unusual, but it was safe and solved the problem of their child reaching for the ornaments or trying to pull the tree over. Other parents have found it useful to put their Christmas tree inside a playpen to provide an instant security fence, keeping children away from the tree.

When Lane was very small, Kathy and I bought a little tree and placed it on top of a table, out of his reach. It's important for parents to recognize the obvious. Little children ages one to two are fascinated by Christmas trees and will naturally gravitate towards one. Instead of trying to change the child's natural and almost impossible-to-control curiosity towards a tree, it's easier to change our plans, since the tree will be up for only a few weeks. At most you'll probably have to deal with this particular problem once or twice. Remember to use caution when other small children come over after yours are bigger and your tree is out.

Talking

About the same time children are learning to walk they begin talking. As with walking, they'll make lots of mistakes while learning to talk. Be patient and allow them room for trial and error. When a child mispronounces a word, either say nothing or answer by using the word correctly. Stuttering frequently begins from an over emphasis on correct speech. If you're patient, there's less chance that stuttering problems will develop.

If your child starts to stutter, be patient and avoid looking directly at your child because that seems to heighten the tension and anxiety. If your child keeps balking, say, "When you think of the answer later, will you tell me?"

When children are learning to speak they will often point and whine for attention when they already know the word they want to use, such as "milk." When you see your child begin to do this and realize he is pointing rather than speaking, act as if you don't understand and say, "I'm not sure what you want but I'm sure you do. Say the right word, please." Of course your child will get frustrated and may have a minor fit at first, but if you're patient, most children will soon start saying the right word again.

Fussing

Fussing is a problem for all children at some time. When children are tired, worn out and ready for a nap, fussing sometimes keeps them awake. (Remember, small children hate to give in to a nap.) Fussing can become chronic. In that case it needs to be nipped in the bud before it becomes a habit. Parents could tune out their children's complaints, forcing one of two general reactions: (1) child feeling ignored and unloved or (2) child increasing volume and sometimes increasing frequency.

Either way, the parents end up the loser. When children fuss, tell them, "That's fussing and you must stop or else you can go to the time-out corner and say, 'fuss-fuss-fuss' until the timer goes off." If your child continues to fuss, then allow him the opportunity to fuss in the corner.

Toilet Training

A typical time to begin thinking about toilet training is about 18-30 months of age. No doubt you'll hear lots of advice from well-meaning friends and relatives who want to impose their advice on you. Avoid letting them do so, because toilet training is up to your child and you. Here are some major considerations:

First, your child must be old enough and strong enough to sit unsupported on a child's potty or the commode. If he can't sit unsupported, then he's definitely not ready. If he's too scared to sit on the commode, then don't force the issue and try again in a few weeks.

Second, your child will need to have an incentive to want to begin toilet training, such as a desire to stop wearing diapers, or becoming a "big boy/girl" like Johnny or Christy. One advantage of enrolling a child in a Sunday School or Mother's Day Out program is the opportunity to see other children using a toilet and wanting to be able to because of what they see.

Third, parents must be willing to stop whatever they are doing and spend the time necessary to go to the toilet with their child when the need is expressed. This will mean interrupting conversations, meals and shopping trips. Unless you and your child are ready for these three considerations then don't even attempt toilet training.

During this training period children frequently become fascinated with public restrooms. They'll say they need to go to the bathroom; once there, they will look around and then ask to leave. You may think your child has developed some strange preoccupations with public restrooms, since every time you sit down to a meal in a restaurant your child has to "go potty." Stay calm; "this too shall pass." Once children learn the location and arrangement of public restrooms, their fascination tends to diminish. It's simply a way children learn about their world, and it's an important part of their education. After all, one of their fears as they begin toilet training is that they'll have an accident, so going to the restroom on a dry run is like practicing for a fire drill. It's a good preventative step for your child and you, so cooperate like a good sport.

If Your Child Has an Accident

First, never, *never* shame a child for having an accident. He's not a "bad boy" for a slip up, so don't say it. We adults have accidents of one sort or another, and no one calls us "bad grown-ups" when we make mistakes. Second, shaming a child because of any accidental behavior whether it be toilet training, stuttering or being clumsy tends to add to the anxiety and may make your child more likely to have another accident the next time.

When your child wets or soils himself, simply clean up the mess with as little fuss as possible. Reassure the child with, "No big deal, I used to have accidents when I was your age, too." Then go about business as usual. If you reassure children and minimize the effects of accidents, they'll reward you with more self-confident behavior and fewer accidents.

Using a Star Chart

We used a Star Chart (see next page) and a set of rules to help Lane become toilet trained. We began using the system when he was about 2 1/2 years old. After one month Lane was basically trained, with only an occasional accident. We taped charts to the refrigerator at his eye level and purchased stars at a variety store. As Lane earned stars he got to stick them on the chart. Completed charts containing two rows of five stars each could be used for a trip to McDonald's or exchanged for $1 toward the purchase of a pair of cowboy boots. Lane put the stars on his chart as he earned them. After he was trained we continued to use the charts for several months and then gradually phased them out.

Star Chart

Rules: "You will get one star for urinating and two stars for a bowel movement. If you have a dry diaper and pants when you wake up you will get two more stars. When you have stars in all the boxes in both rows, you can go to McDonald's (or some similar treat). If you go to bed wearing training pants but wake up wet in the morning, you'll have to wear diapers to help stay dry the next night. If you wake up with a dry diaper the next morning, you can try training pants again."

Note: Instead of telling all the rules to Lane at once, we repeated portions of them, when appropriate, to encourage him each time he earned another star. At first each chart contained two rows of five boxes each, for a total of 10. Each time Lane had a successful trip to the bathroom or a dry night, he earned one to three stars which were placed in one box. Soon he could fill several boxes with stars each day. As Lane became more proficient and completed charts rapidly, we increased the number of boxes from 10 to 12, then to 14. He never seemed to notice or complain about the increase. Had he done so, we would have explained that it was necessary to "raise the price" because the rows had become so easy to complete.

THE TEMPORARY TWOS

Most of you have already heard about the Terrible Twos — that period from about 18 months of age to around 3 years. Let me tell you about Robin.

Robin's father, Ralph, is still in shock. This cute little two-year-old has made an unforgettable impression on everyone who knows her. Her trail of disasters began with the toilet. Alice the cat got dunked, drowned and flushed. A few days later Robin decided to give teddy bear a bath— she set him on top of the heating element in the dishwasher. The bear came out a limp crispy critter.

Robin then attacked the refrigerator. She stuck some magnetic letters in the vents just before the family took a weekend trip, causing the motor to burn out.

Next day Robin's mother left her asleep in her car seat while she went in the post office to mail a letter. When she came out she discovered Robin driving the car straight into a tree.

A week later Robin's mom and dad parked their car halfway in the garage after a shopping trip because they were planning to unload groceries. Robin was strapped in the car seat, and her mother had the keys. While the parents were in the kitchen they heard loud noises from the garage. When they got outside they found the automatic garage door bouncing up and down on the hood of the car with you know who inside pushing the button. Within just a few weeks Robin's damages cost $2,296.37. She is a prime example of the "Temporary Twos."

The good news is that this is a time-limited phase and usually disappears around a child's third birthday. Robin's parents will celebrate that birthday with a sigh of relief.

Tantrums

One of the major symptoms of the temporary twos is the tantrums that children throw at any and all places, especially grocery stores and when we have company. Usually the tantrum is a result of the child's not getting his way. Tantrums usually get a child a lot of negative attention. Tantrums can be compared to the comedy routines of Bob Hope, Bill Cosby and Carol Burnett. All three are comedians, with distinctly different kinds of humor, but they all have one thing in common: "When the Audience Walks Out, the Clown Stops the Act." And that's what a tantrum is, an act on your child's part to pressure you to give in. The best way to respond when your child tries to bluff you is to call the bluff firmly but quickly.

If the tantrum takes place while you have company present, tell your child, "I have a feeling you're acting up on purpose in front of my guest, so go to your time-out corner for three minutes. If you keep up the fit you will have to practice it the entire time-out time." Tell your guest, "I'm sorry about that, but we're having to stop this routine in order to make things better."

Public Demonstrations

In the supermarket a man was pushing a grocery cart which contained a screaming, yelling, bellowing two-year-old. The gentleman kept repeating such admonitions as "Don't get excited, Albert," "Don't scream, Albert," "Don't yell, Albert."

A woman standing next to him said, "You certainly are to be commended for trying to soothe your son Albert."

The man looked at her and said soberly, "Lady, *I'm* Albert!"

If you're in the supermarket and your child starts the "I wants!" say, "Look at me; I came here to shop, not to listen to your fussing. Stop it now or next time you'll stay at home. Think seriously about babysitting for your children during shopping. You might begin a shoppers' Baby-sitting Co-op.

Kathy and I had just settled down for a nice meal in a restaurant when Lane decided to start acting up. After an appropriate warning, we surprised him by putting him in time-out, a corner near our table where we could watch him at all times. One waiter walked by and said, "Hello, little boy. What are you doing here?" Lane's expression and our dirty looks were all he needed to decide to move on. By having called Lane's bluff in public one time, all we needed to do in future situations was give this warning: "You had better knock off that routine real quick or we'll put you in time-out right over there. Remember the last time?" Once was sufficient proof for Lane.

Unfortunately, many parents feel years of empty threats and hours of yelling are a more humane way of dealing with the tantrum. I'm convinced just the opposite is true.

Another consideration about taking children to public places is to remember the reality of the child's age and the setting. Most children under 30 months of age just aren't ready to sit through a long meal, so to avoid frustration, either go to a fast food restaurant or get a baby-sitter when you want to go out for a big meal.

Where Do They Learn That?

Ah, those two-year-olds. Just about the time you think you've conquered the temporary twos they surprise you with their insight into human emotions. Once when Lane was barely two years old we were eating dinner. He was still upset at being disciplined, so he looked me straight in the eye and said, "I'll never speak to you again!" Where did those words come from? He had only been speaking in sentences for a few months. I guess sentences like that are handed down, generation to generation, on the playgrounds, in the church nurseries and in day care centers across America. They come to kids mysteriously, like the rules to "Hide-and-Seek."

A few weeks after that episode Lane threatened to "run away."

"I'd hate to see you do that, Son. Have you thought about your toys?"

"Huh? What do you mean?"

"Well, if you're going to leave here, you won't be able to take all your toys with you, and we won't need them. So do you want me to give them to one of your friends?"

He thought about that for a few minutes and decided, "I think I'll stay." Then we solved the problem together.

These surprising little moments are what help parents and kids survive the temporary twos — with joy!

TYPICAL CHILDHOOD FEARS

Toddlers naturally develop some common fears. They may end up fearing something that strikes us as a "silly thing to fear," but it's still a very real fear to them. Some typical fears are:

- [ ] Their parents are lost forever when they are out of sight.

- [ ] The vacuum cleaner will run over them.

- [ ] The shampoo will hurt "real bad" if it gets in their eyes.

- [ ] They will slip down the bathtub drain or disappear down the toilet.

- [ ] There are monsters in the closet or in the dark.

☐ A haircut is painful because part of their body is cut off and thrown away.

☐ A dog is going to bite them.

Accept the fears as real; remove the child from the fearful situation and talk about the situation. Help him to go back and confront his fears.

Fear of Strangers

Many children develop a strong "stranger anxiety." They hide, cry and sometimes scream when they are around people they don't know. Instead of saying, "There's nothing to be afraid of," briefly explain to your child what's going on: "That's the man who delivers the mail to us. Let's go see what he brought." Or, "That man walking out to our car is going to ask me how much gas I need, and then he'll go behind our car and put the gas nozzle in. You'll probably hear some bumps and rattles as he opens the gas tank." Interpretative remarks like these help children make sense out of new experiences and decrease the likelihood of anxiety occurring next time.

Fear of Separation

While the fear of strangers typically occurs when a child is in a parent's presence, fear of separation is a time of uneasiness that takes place when a child discovers he's been left alone by Mom or Dad. Typically this begins about 18 months of age and decreases between ages two and three. When separation anxiety takes place at home, your child may go from room to room looking for you. It's especially upsetting to parents when they leave their child with a trusted baby-sitter who previously cared for the child successfully, but now Junior has suddenly started to cry and panic.

The best way to handle separation anxiety is to explain to the baby-sitter what's going on. Then tell your child Mommy'll be back, "after you've had dinner," or "after you've gone to bed but before you wake up in the morning." (Give your child something of yours to keep for you while you're gone. This helps assure the child that you'll come back.) Then leave, despite the cries of panic. You almost have to handle this "cold turkey" because all the reassurance in the world will only make your child more fearful and clinging and leave you feeling guilty. Besides, sooner or later your child will have to accept other adults in charge. The sooner he gets adjusted to separating from his parents, the better.

To help your child deal with fears and develop social skills, you can:

- ☐ Invite other children over to play or take your child to playgrounds where he can play with other children.
- ☐ Teach your child to use words instead of fists to protect what is his.
- ☐ Show your child how to share, but don't force it.
- ☐ Begin to teach your child some simple rules.
- ☐ Praise your child when he uses good social behavior.

BABY-SITTERS

The First Sitter

Leaving your child with a sitter for the first time is usually tougher on you than your child. Naturally he's going to cry, and you're going to feel like you're abandoning your child. The concerned parents are fearful of what might happen. The following "How to Prepare the Baby-sitter" list can be a great comfort to the parents as well as to the sitter.

How to Prepare the Baby-sitter

- ☐ Tour the house to locate telephones, exits, first aid supplies, flashlight, play areas.
- ☐ Discuss food habits, bedtime, favorite activities, special appliances, TV rules, medicines, allergies, other health problems.
- ☐ Confirm expected time of return.
- ☐ Make a telephone number list, including where you will be, a neighbor's number, emergency numbers.
- ☐ Make arrangements for the fee you will pay.
- ☐ Point out pad for telephone messages and return numbers.
- ☐ Demonstrate any unusual locks on doors and state policy of locking doors while you're gone.
- ☐ Suggest sitter privileges, such as TV, food, visitors, telephone calls.
- ☐ Write any "special instructions" down so there will be no misunderstanding.

Leaving Baby Overnight

How early is too early to leave a baby with someone while you're gone overnight? That depends on your situation. One physician recommends to new parents that when their newborn is three months old they make arrangements for the baby to be kept by grandparents or trusted friends while they go away for a few days for a second honeymoon. I think that's excellent advice, both for the baby and the parents.

Friends used to ask Kathy and me why we didn't go off more often and leave Lane with a sitter, especially overnight. Our response was, "We waited ten years to have him, he's lots of fun to be with, and we want to be with him." I think if he had been a difficult baby we might have had something different to say. Or, if we had already had several other children, we probably would have jumped at the chance to get away alone.

For whatever reason, if you have a need to get away from your children for a few days, do it. Find some friends or relatives and form a child care co-op. You will sit for their children, and they can take care of yours. If you're not sure how they'll respond to such a deal, offer to take care of their kids first. In essence, you're offering to "pay in advance," so it's easier to make the suggestion.

NOW I HAVE A CHOICE

The first thirty months are times when every parent will feel stressed and a little trapped. Babies take a lot of time and energy, but with Common Sense Discipline you always have options. Knowing you have options helps you get past the rough spots and even the temporary terrible twos.

Knowing what to say and do in specific situations can help you concentrate on enjoying your kids. When parenting is an enjoyable experience, you will naturally be more loving and tolerant. Remember, this book is designed to help, not judge. Nobody is perfect, so hang in there, you're doing fine.

5

Exploring the World
with Limits

3-5 Years

S hortly after turning five, Lane ended a disagreement by
stating, "I want to be adopted!"

He didn't expect my response, "Listen, maybe you
can't stand it here and maybe you don't like me very much.
I understand because sometimes I don't like me either. But
even with the problem we're having right now, *I still love
you, and I always will.* You're my boy, and I'm proud of
you. There's just *no way* I'm ever going to allow you to be
adopted. That's final, so we might as well look for some
ways to get along with each other and start having some
fun again." And we did!

The preschool years are filled with these little
surprises.

Chart 3 pictures a little more freedom of choice for the
preschooler within the fences of the parent's decisions.
Young children from three to five years old are wondering
wanderers. They love to explore, touch, watch and taste
almost anything. Their daily adventures are fun to watch,
and conversation is a joy. Give them lots of choices—

Common Sense Discipline Chart 3

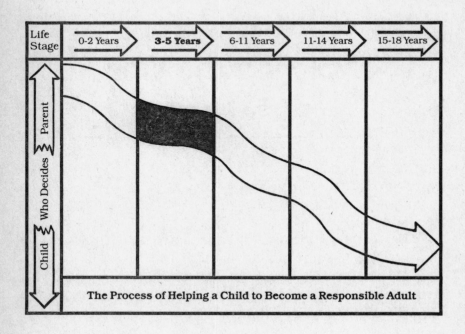

choices of colors, sizes, shapes, foods, activities, etc. But, remember, you still call the shots. You're the one who trains the vine. You see the future; they only see today.

Keep Talking

The years from three to five are fascinating for parents. Simple conversations become trips into fantasyland. Learning to use words to tell about what's happening inside us is stimulating to most youngsters. At times it's entertaining to listen to the three- to five-year-old tell about life from his perspective.

Not all talk is designed to be an exchange of information. Sometimes you will use conversation to help your child discover something new. These discovery talks will require time and a willingness to let the conversation flow and wander. During these talks both parent and child will discover things and set themselves up for similar talks in the future.

At times we just want to hear about feelings. When feelings are negative, our first tendency will be to try to "fix it"—to make it better. The most important thing we can do in a feeling conversation is to just listen. A preschooler has lots of different feelings. He just doesn't have as many words to use to describe his feelings.

During the 1950's, Art Linkletter demonstrated the ability to talk with preschoolers about discoveries, feelings and other surprises. One of the keys to his success was his ability to get the kids to talk about their pretend thoughts. He would ask the kids to tell their innermost wishes, to talk about what kind of animal they'd like to be, and to announce what ages they'd prefer to be and why. You never knew when one of those talks would make your day.

Art Linkletter tells the story of a little boy who listened attentively to his Sunday School teacher tell about a familiar Bible passage. She read, "From dust thou art and to dust thou shalt return." The little boy's mind captured that phrase, and as soon as he got home, he looked under his bed and ran to his mother.

"Mom, is it true that God makes people out of dust?"

"Yes," Mom said.

"Mom, is it true that we're dust after we're dead?"

"Yes, why?"

"Well, go look under my bed, quick! Somebody's either coming or going!"

The three- to five-year-old will sometimes mix up the facts. For instance, kids have rewritten the lyrics of some famous songs. Have you heard these new song lyrics?

> "I'm going to Alabama with a band-aid on my
>   knee."
> "Gladly, the cross-eyed bear"
> "Stand beside her, and guide her, with the light
>   through the night from a bulb."

Don't spend your time correcting. Tune in and listen. Learn to enjoy the expression of life.

Parent Preparation

At first, children will overgeneralize; they may see a cat, cow or collie and call each one a "doggy." Avoid the temptation to make too many corrections. They'll soon make their own modifications. Gradually your children will learn to play cooperatively and share with others. Noticing these achievements and sharing your feelings will assure their reassurance. ("I liked the way you played with Betty and shared your toys with her.") Sharing and cooperation are important skills for the youngsters to repeat over and over during this period. And patience is a skill you'll need to practice over and over. Relax with your children. Enjoy life; it's not time to rush and push.

As you do things together, talk out loud about your thoughts. "Let's see; I can tell it's cold outside by the frost on the window. So I'll want to put on my coat to stay warm when I go outside." These words help your child to learn how to think through situations.

Crayons or felt tip markers will eventually draw masterpieces on your walls, furniture and/or clothes. Many children will use these colors to mark their rooms.

If asked, "Why did you do that?" they will invariably respond, "I don't know."

Try to channel the coloring activity to a more acceptable surface. Firmly say, "Here, I know you like your pretty colors. From now on only color in your coloring book or on plain paper. If you color on the wall or something other than your paper, you'll have to go to time-out."

When your child brings you his artwork, avoid saying, "What is this?" Instead say, "There are lots of pretty colors here. Tell me about your drawing," or "Thanks for taking the time to draw me a picture. I appreciate your thinking of me," or "This looks great—tell me about it." During the child's early years it's important for parents to spend time with their child. Do things with the child—have fun. These hours of time will be an investment in the future. Try doing the following activities with your child:

- ☐ Going for a walk
- ☐ Reading a story
- ☐ Wrestling in the floor
- ☐ Being silly
- ☐ Working a puzzle
- ☐ Taking pictures
- ☐ Going for a ride
- ☐ Singing songs
- ☐ Looking at the family album

Regardless of how you decide to spend the time, try to invest a minimum of 15-30 minutes a day with each child. Sound simple? Time yourself for one week! Keep a daily record. You may be surprised.

Remain Flexible

I goofed up one morning. Kathy had Lane's lunch box all ready for nursery school, and I was taking him. Just as he was about to get out of the car, I realized he'd forgotten his lunch box. Even mean old me isn't yet ready to let a five-year-old miss lunch, especially since he had a very light breakfast.

"I'll go get your lunch box and bring it back. You go on in to school."

"I want to ride home with you and then come back."

By this time his teacher was holding the car door open, and other parents were lined up in their cars, waiting to drop their children off.

"No, son, you go on in to school, and I'll bring your lunch to you."

"Please let me go with you, Dad," and he started to tear up.

By then I was getting uptight because I thought he was stalling. Here was my kid arguing with me.

"You can do it the easy way or the hard way, son, but either way you're going on in to school," I said *firmly*.

With tears in his eyes and a dirty look on his face, he went inside. As I was driving back home to get his lunch box, it occurred to me what the fuss was all about. Lane simply wanted to be with me; nursery school was not the issue. In my rush to get things done "right," I lost sight of the fact that this was nursery school; they don't give you detentions or fail you for being late. The real issue was that my son wanted to spend some more time with me.

What would have happened if he had stayed with me in the car while I returned for his lunch box? He would have missed about 20 minutes of nursery school, we would have avoided an unnecessary confrontation, and we could have spent more of that special time together.

Sometimes it's easy to get the cart before the horse in this parenting business. While trying to be straightforward and in charge, I became bound by my own system. As your child grows up, remember: *"It's always important to be flexible.*" The world won't come to an end just because your routine needs to be modified.

TRAVELING WITH SMALL CHILDREN

A little planning can ease the tension of traveling with a small child. Try:

- Putting together a car activity bag with books, paper, stickers, card games, a cassette recorder and favorite tapes, a special treat or a surprise toy.
- Giving each child a small "Trip Treats" bag. Then each time the kids fight or argue, each of them is to give you one treat out of their bags. At the end of the trip, the remaining treats are theirs to keep.
- Assembling a snack kit for the car. You should include a plastic cup, a small spoon, a bib, Wet-Ones, crackers, fruit, a dry wash cloth and a few small trash bags.
- Planning rest stops about every two hours.
- Letting off energy and getting the circulation going by doing impromptu exercises at a roadside park.
- Try not to travel more than eight hours in a day.

WHEN PARENTS ARE GONE FOR THE NIGHT

At times a parent will have to be gone overnight. Make preparations for the child before you leave by:

1. Recording at least one story for each night you'll be away. On a cassette tape read from one of your child's favorite books so he can follow along. Hear-

ing an absent parent's voice is reassuring. At the end of the story say, "Goodnight, I'll see you again at home in __days."

2. If possible, have a relative or trusted sitter care for the child in your home to minimize a change in surroundings and routine. If the child is taken to a relative's home, write out a familiar routine and let your child bring one bag of toys.

3. Whatever the reason for leaving, tell your child, "A mommy's supposed to come back for her child, and I'll come back to you, too." After you return, remind your child, "Remember that I said I'd come back? Well, here I am." This kind of experience builds your child's confidence that absences aren't forever. Naturally the routine of bringing home a special gift doesn't hurt, but you need to be cautious or else your child will come to expect the "gift" out of habit.

TATTLING

When your child begins tattling try this, "There are two things that you should tattle about. Remember them:

1. Tell me anytime someone might get hurt doing what they are doing. It's OK to tell me, even if you get called names.

2. Tell me anytime someone might hurt you.

You may be tempted to tell about other kinds of things, but just remember our two rules."

ARE YOU READY FOR PETS?

Here's where Kathy and I really made a mistake. When Lane was three years old the subject of pets came up, and we mentioned that "one day" we'd get him a dog. Right away he started saying, "How soon?" So Kathy said, "Next year, when you're four years old." Four years old sounded like a long time, but kids never forget. When the long awaited birthday arrived, the "hounding" began, "Where's my dog you promised?"

Fortunately for us, Lane's birthday came in November so we could say with good conscience, "We need to wait until spring when the weather is warm enough for your dog to stay outside at night." Lane gave in, but soon it was time to fulfill our promise.

One spring evening we bought a cute little female beagle. "Sparky" was her name. She was 100% dog and I don't think she ever slept. The first morning Lane ran outside to play with his new dog. Both Sparky and he were excited at first, but soon Lane lost interest. All Sparky wanted to do was jump up on Lane, knocking him over. Within 3 days Lane avoided going into the backyard to play. The logical consequence was that Sparky got less and less attention from the entire family. Whenever someone dared venture into the backyard, she would go crazy. No one wanted to be around a "hyper" dog, regardless of how cute she was. This cycle continued for about two months.

Allowing Sparky to come home with us was a mistake. When you realize you've made a mistake, do what we tell our children to do: Admit the mistake, and correct it as best you can. I told Lane I had decided to advertise Sparky for sale to a good home.

"But she's my dog, and you promised me."

"That's right, son, and we've all given this a good try, but it's just not working out the way we had planned. Sparky's losing out, too. She needs a good home where she's wanted, and let's face it, she's getting lonely. It's unfair to Sparky to keep her when we aren't a good family for her. So I'm going to make the decision to find her a good home where she'll be welcomed."

I placed the ad that afternoon: "For Sale: frisky beagle" (At least I warned them). Now Sparky is the wife of Jack the Beagle. They live in the country with lots of room where I'm sure it's best for all concerned. Deciding to sell Sparky was a tough decision, but at that time for us it was a right one.

MANAGING AGGRESSION

During the early childhood years, parents are often surprised with sudden bursts of aggression in the youngsters. We find ourselves wondering where such a sweet child gets this preoccupation with fighting and hitting. Around age three many children go through a bug-squashing phase in which any and all ants, worms and caterpillars they come across are subject to being flattened on sight. Sometimes a child will try to flatten another child. Usually, just feelings are hurt. Avoid making too big of a deal about it. Try the following:

Biting

When biting gets out of hand, you might use negative practice by sending your child to a time-out corner and have him bite down on a washrag for three minutes until the timer goes off. Some people will tell you to encourage the injured child to bite back, but that only teaches that one bad turn deserves another instead of eliminating future biting. Punish the guilty party; don't teach the innocent how to be a biter.

Fussing and Fighting

Fussing and fighting are typical problems common to almost all small children. If they never fussed, we should wonder what was wrong with them. As long as the fussing and fighting are about the normal childhood things and at normal levels, I suggest letting kids solve their own problems without adults getting involved. Occasionally things will get out of hand, and you'll need to step in.

A low intensity situation is demonstrated by arguing or verbal fighting. Whenever two children are fussing back and forth and the noise level gets out of hand or the threats become a little too vivid, simply say, "Look, I don't know what all the fussing and arguing is about, but I do know I don't like the noise. I'll tell you what—you have one minute to settle this yourselves quietly and work out your own solution. If you don't settle this in one minute, I'm going to come back in here and give you my solution. And I guarantee you won't like my solution. Now you have one minute to settle this quietly." Then walk out of the room.

Most children will quickly come up with some creative solutions if you just offer them the opportunity to do so and make it uncomfortable if they don't. It doesn't matter if one decides to yield to the other and "give in," because yielding is useful to learn early in life, especially before kids start riding their bikes in the street. Don't worry about yielding becoming lopsided. If it does and one child does all the yielding, pretty soon he'll get tired of it and will insist on reciprocity.

If your kids don't solve their problem after one minute and are still arguing, simply come in and give them your solution which might be, "Time-out for you in that corner, and time-out for you over there." If they continue to fuss or nag, say, "I'm adding one minute for each time you fuss." Then walk out after setting the timer.

Fist Fights and Wrestling

A high intensity situation is identified by physical fighting. It can be handled by making your child shadow box in a corner or hold weights or rocks for three minutes. (The arms will get tired *real* fast.) Most will be worn out before the time is up. If one of the two says, "It wasn't my fault," tell him, "You need to learn to avoid getting into fights. Just because someone dares you to fight is no reason to fight back. This way I make sure the one responsible is punished." If you are certain that one child deliberately goaded the other into a fight, you might give the guilty party a double portion of shadow boxing, while the other gets a regular portion for fighting back. One punch in self-defense is one thing; a prolonged fight is another.

Some parents think they should let the kids fight it out to the end. You use your judgment. You may find a tooth gone and a few bruises. Other parents believe if one child hits another the innocent should be able to hit the guilty one back twice. The problem with that is the same as biting back. Besides, the innocent party will rarely hit the guilty one hard enough to do any good. Usually the innocent are too shy, intimidated or afraid to take the necessary action. The shadow box routine is more useful.

PLAYING SICK

Children sometimes use illness and complaints of being sick to avoid doing something they don't want to do. It's a convenient excuse to keep from leaving a parent's side or going to Sunday School or nursery school. When you feel that your child is faking and his temperature and other signs look all right, respond to his complaints this way: "If you're really sick, I understand, and of course you don't have to go. If you are too sick to go to nursery school, then you'll need to stay in your pajamas all day so you can rest and get well and go back to school soon.

"The only exceptions to staying in bed will be to go to the bathroom and to come to the table to eat, if you feel like it. If you get to feeling better after school lets out, you'll still need to stay in bed and rest to avoid a 'relapse' just in case." If the child is faking, you will find him getting well—fast!

RELIEVING FEARS

Technically speaking, many of the common childhood fears might be considered phobias. While they may be irrational or highly unlikely to come true ("there's a bear in my room"), to the child these are real events, and making light of such fears is counterproductive. Parents can help children overcome any fear by teaching them ways to solve their own problems.

If your child is afraid of outside noises, avoid saying, "They're only noises." Instead, explain what makes the noise, "When the wind blows the tree and the tree rubs against the house, it sounds like this," and show the child how such a noise is produced by rubbing two of his toys together. If possible, take your child outside, "Would you like to go see how the tree makes that noise?" If your child is too scared to do so, practice making the noise. Show him how he can make the noise by mimicking it. Once he can produce a similar sound, he'll have more control over it.

One night Lane was scared of shadows in his room. He had a lamp with a clown on the base, and it did cast an ominous shadow when turned a certain way. So we rotated the lamp half a turn and then practiced making shadow figures with our hands on the wall. "When you think of a shadow, let it be a signal to close your eyes and think of going to a fun place like Disneyland or the beach. That way you can use the shadow for a signal to have make-believe fun."

Since most children's fears are based on imaginary facts, an imaginary solution will often work. When Lane was convinced that there was a bear in his bedroom, I asked him if he would rather shoot it or hit it over the head and knock it out. "I want to shoot it," he said.

"Okay, here are two of your guns. Here is your pop-gun rifle, and here is your cowboy gun. Which one do you want to use?" He looked at me with a funny expression, but when he saw that I was taking him seriously, he selected the pop-gun.

"Okay, hold it real steady. Can you see the bear over there?" I pointed.

"Yes, Daddy."

"Okay, wait 'til you have him sighted, and then aim and shoot." Bang. "Looks like you got him. Can you see him anymore?"

"No, Daddy."

"Okay, if you ever need to shoot a bear again, Son, you know what to do." To this day I don't think we've had another unwanted bear in our house.

Nightmares

All children have bad dreams from time to time. Persistent bad dreams or nightmares may come from a friend who tells scary stories. It may have been some bad news on TV (and there's plenty of that). Or, it may have been any number of circumstances. It's useless to tell a child, "It's all in your head." That's just the point—our dreams are in our head. The child knows it, and he becomes scared of going to sleep because he fears another nightmare. It's rather like an adult who is reluctant to take a boat ride because he gets seasick easily. There's some justification for the reluctance.

Your child may need you to wait in his room for several nights until he goes to sleep. I discourage rocking an older child, over two years of age, to sleep because it can become a habit, making rocking necessary for sleep. Lying on a pallet beside your child's bed until he goes to sleep can be helpful. Lane likes this occasionally if he's having trouble sleeping. He's almost grown out of the need for it, but it's important that he knows I'll lie down beside him if he needs me to. It hardly ever takes more than 15 minutes until he's asleep, and it gives us a chance to relax and talk quietly together. It's a small thing to do that can comfort him a lot.

If your child's nightmares haven't diminished after two weeks of using these suggestions, or if he frequently wakes up screaming, professional intervention is probably called for. Ask your child's pediatrician for advice about what to do next.

Serious Illness

I once worked with a child whose father had been hospitalized unexpectedly with severe health problems. Eight-year-old Joey was told nothing about the nature of his father's illness, only that Dad was taken by ambulance to the hospital for several weeks. During that time, the rest of the family walked on pins and needles lest they upset and scare Joey.

Unfortunately, their behavior did exactly that. It was obvious to Joey that something was going on, and for some reason his relatives weren't leveling with him. He decided something must have been very wrong with his father because no one bothered to tell him.

When a close relative is in the hospital or when someone dies, it is imperative for parents to tell their children the truth in a manner appropriate to the child's age and understanding. A rule of thumb is this: If a child is old enough to formulate a question, then he's old enough to receive an appropriate answer. Gory details should be omitted, but a simple, straightforward answer will work wonders for a child's peace of mind. *Not* knowing is almost always worse than knowing. If a child is patronized or ignored during a time of sickness or sorrow, he'll assume that he may be at fault or that things are worse. Then his fears will really skyrocket, like Joey's did. Even small children have a fairly high tolerance for bad news if it's presented to them fairly, accurately and without undue alarm.

Typically children in this predicament assume the worst possible outcome. Rarely do I see children who erroneously concluded the best possible outcome. Tell children the truth on a level they can understand. Avoid fancy terms and jargon. Just say, "He's really sick," instead of "He has spinal meningitis."

When Someone Dies

Children growing up today are more aware of the reality of death than you may realize, yet most parents shy away from discussing the end of life. Youngsters need simple and honest information about what has happened when someone dies. The real facts will almost always be better than the fantasies dreamed up out of ignorance.

Making sure kids get good information reminds me of the story of Jimmy and his baby sister. Late one night Jimmy's little sister was rushed to the hospital in one of those cars with flashing red lights. Dad woke Jimmy up, and they followed the ambulance to the emergency room. There, after several tests, the doctor said that Jimmy's sister needed a blood transfusion. She had a very rare blood type, the same as Jimmy's. Dad bent down and asked if Jimmy would be willing to help his sister by giving her some of his blood. Jimmy looked stunned but eager, "Sure, Dad, I'll do it."

Dad returned to the doctor, and Jimmy turned to his mother and said, "Here, you keep my bear; I won't need it anymore. I'm going to give Sis my blood. I love you, Mommy." Jimmy thought giving blood meant he would have to die. He didn't have enough information, and what he had he didn't understand.

Preparing your child for the funeral or the memorial service is extremely important even if the child does not attend. Explaining death and funerals and cemeteries to your child helps to dispel his fear and worry.

Don't tell your child that Granny died because God needed another angel. Your youngster may wonder why God needed his Granny. After all, God's got thousands of angels, and he's only got *one* Granny.

Don't use words like "sleep" or "gone away" as an attempt to soften the harshness of death. These euphemisms will cause the child to fantasize about the loved one's return. When you are faced with the task of helping a three- to five-year-old through the grief process, remember:

- ☐ Shoot straight with the youngster. He will sense something wrong sooner than you think.

- ☐ Tell the child as soon as it is appropriate; don't wait until the rest of the family has recovered. The child shouldn't have to grieve alone.

- ☐ Talk about good memories of the deceased.

- ☐ Hug your child a lot.

- ☐ Use simple but factual information in describing what happens or might happen at the funeral and cemetery.

- ☐ Don't be afraid to cry. It's good to cry. Death is a sad time.

Security Blankets

Like Linus of Peanuts fame, many children get attached to a blanket, favorite stuffed toy or pillow which they drag with them everywhere. These items become like a part of the child's body. Removing the blanket would be as painful as removing an arm; at least it seems that way.

This security blanket can become a major source of parental concern. "But what if she still wants it by the time she goes to school?" The point is, the blanket offers some degree of comfort and security or else it wouldn't be that important to the child to lug around everywhere. As long as it's offering that much comfort, I wouldn't try to get rid of it.

If you feel your child is about ready to give up the blanket but just doesn't know how to let go, make it easier for her. Suggest an alternate place to put the freshly laundered blanket, like in the linen closet. I know it's probably in shreds, but it is precious to your child and hard to let go of. Offer to clean it up, put it in a special plastic bag or box where she'll know it'll be safe from moths and where she can take it out or look at it anytime she might want to. Tell her it's starting to get worn and she might want to save it for her little girl or her little girl's dolls someday.

If that doesn't work, simply allow logical consequences to take place and let her take the blanket to kindergarten. Either a teacher will tell her it's against the rules and she'll probably comply, or the other kids will make enough fun of her for being a baby that she'll leave the blanket at home after a few days.

Thumb Sucking

Thumb sucking seems to embarrass and irritate parents more than the sight of a security blanket. Like security blankets, it's usually a bigger problem for parents than for the child. If yours is still sucking his thumb and you think it's time for him to stop, you might ask if he's ready to stop now or if he wants to stop before school starts. If he's ready now, ask him if he wants you to remind him when he has his thumb in is mouth or would he rather receive stars on a chart for each time you see his mouth empty? If neither of these approaches works, I'd let logical consequences take their course.

Most thumb sucking is taken care of in the first 3-4 days of school by the other kids' taunts. If he's willing to withstand their ridicule, then the thumb must have precious security value for him, so I probably wouldn't try to take it away. Besides, I know lots of adults who suck on cigarettes; a thumb is much safer.

BEDTIME PROBLEMS

Sooner or later all children will try to get in their parents' bed. Besides the security it offers, the parents' bed is usually warmer and has more room than the child's. Crawling in a parent's bed on Saturday mornings to snuggle is one thing, but it's not a good idea for children to sleep overnight in their parents' bed, even when one parent is gone. It's too easy for this to become a habit, and then the child will have trouble sleeping in his own bed. After a while, children who sleep in their parents' bed confuse their role in relation to their parents and may demand to remain in that bed, resenting the parent (usually Dad) who expects them to sleep in their own bed.

One way to encourage your child to sleep in his own bed is to offer him a star or check mark for each morning you wake up and find him in his own bed. It works even better if you let him make the marks. When he has earned five stars, let him select a special treat worth about one dollar. As he becomes more and more proficient at remaining in his own bed, increase the price for the treat from five to seven stars then to ten, etc.

Finally, phase the program out when the child has developed the habit of staying in his own bed. Of course, waking up in his own bed means your child did not go into your room the night before and have to be brought back to bed by you. In such a case, he doesn't get a star the next morning. If he asks why not, explain why. This procedure has worked quite well for a number of parents.

Nightly Routines

It helps to have an established routine each night. One family used an old-fashioned wind-up alarm clock, the kind with two bells on top. It was called Mr. Clock, and whenever bedtime drew near the parents called out, "It's time to wind up Mr. Clock." Their kids raced to be the first one to wind up Mr. Clock. Each got a turn winding the alarm key. Then their parents set the alarm to go off in about 10 minutes. The children knew from experience they only had a brief amount of time to brush their teeth, get a last-minute book or toy, get a hug and kiss from Mom and Dad and then off to bed.

When Mr. Clock's alarm went off, ready or not there was no further running around, but "Off to bed you go." Mom and Dad came in with them to say prayers and tuck them in. I saw that delightful routine in their home on a number of occasions, and it remains the most pleasant bedtime schedule I've ever witnessed.

Routines and rituals are important for children. The more you establish a set time and routine for going to bed, the easier it will be for your children and you. At first it takes practice and patience to establish the routines, but they're well worth the effort.

The main thing about bedtime and naptime for preschool children is that your child stays in bed quietly without disturbing the rest of the family. If you allow her the freedom to read or talk quietly to her sister or stuffed animals, most will soon relax and fall asleep in about 15 minutes.

Distractions at Bedtime

Occasionally a child will have such a large collection of stuffed animals on the bed that sleeping seems impossible. Before you intervene and remove the animals, ask yourself, "Does she seem to sleep in a restful manner, and does she seem rested when she wakes up?" If so, there's probably no problem. Some of us can't imagine how others can sleep on a waterbed or an extra firm bed, but many do. On the other hand, if your child is obviously not rested when she wakes up, start reducing the number of animals she's allowed in bed by one each night until she wakes up rested.

Tell her, "Tonight you can have 11 animals (or whatever number you want to start with), in bed with you." First, remove the three-foot gorilla or any others that are huge. If she doesn't wake up rested the next morning, keep reducing the number by one each night until she does. In less than a week you'll probably have the number down pat. If she refuses to select which animals she wants to start with, tell her, "All right, since you seem to have trouble choosing, I'll make the selection for you." Be sure to leave her favorites with her. Don't allow any trades to be made, or she'll just delay you in a trade-off game to prolong going to bed.

Something that really helps at bedtime is to avoid any activity that gets a child wound up, like wrestling, tickling or playing chase. Choose slow-down activities instead, like reading bedtime books, softly singing gentle songs and saying prayers together. Make sure the TV is off and the lights are turned down. Leave the night-light on and have the bed ready for your child. If you choose to read books, decide how many to let your child select, and then it's time for bed.

WHEN PARENTS DISAGREE

Parents often ask me about being consistent with children. How important is consistency? It would be nice if parents always agreed on everything, but that just doesn't happen. It makes more sense for each parent to be as consistent as possible in his/her own form of discipline so kids will learn predictability.

It can be very helpful to work through a disagreement in front of your children and let them see a solution process, *unless* the problem is about your personal life or something that's clearly not the children's business. When the problem at hand has to do with them, they can watch and even be included in the discussion if it's appropriate.

When Lane first heard Kathy and me arguing about something, he'd get upset and tell us, "Stop arguing, stop arguing."

I'd kneel down beside him and say, "Son, Mom and Dad have a problem right now that we need to work out. We're going to talk about it until we get a good solution. You can stay here and listen, but not interrupt us, or you can play in your room or in the backyard. Either way, we'll keep working on this problem until we have a happy solution."

When children hear parents disagree behind closed doors and then later come out with a "solution," all they may learn is that parents are supposed to "hide" when they have problems. You can't hide your feelings. All children are perceptive and somewhat intuitive. They sense the disturbance in your heart, and they will always imagine the worst. It's best to let them observe two mature adults creating a solution.

A TYPICAL DAY WITH COMMON SENSE DISCIPLINE

Here are some typical situations where Common Sense Discipline can be applied:

Getting Up: "If you get up, get dressed and eat breakfast in a good mood, you'll get one star on your chart. When you have five stars you can have a dollar or pick a toy that costs that much."

After Breakfast: "I enjoyed breakfast with you. It was fun talking about our plans for the day. Now please go wash your hands and face, and then we will play one game together."

"I want to play now, Mommy."

"No, you know your routine. After you eat, you wash your hands and face; then we play. Now hop to it!"

When it comes time to stop playing a game, children often have a hard time quitting abruptly, so give notice like: "I can take three more turns, and then I'll need to go back to my work. You can keep playing here, or you can join me in the kitchen." Count the remaining turns out loud, "That's one...that's two..." and then return to your work.

Later That Morning: "I'm ready for a little break. I sure appreciate the way you've been playing quietly and letting me do my work. That sure does help me. How about we play one of your games for a few minutes now?"

Lunchtime: "When you finish your lunch you can have dessert." *Note*: This doesn't mean lick the plate clean, just a normal portion of food.

"But I don't want to eat this food."

"That's fine. Only eat it if you want dessert."

"But I want my dessert now."

"No, and if you nag me again you'll have to go stand in the time-out corner for three minutes and say 'nag-nag-nag' until the timer goes off.

Nap time: "We have time for one story or one quiet game before nap time. You can pick. When we're finished it will be time to take a nap."

After Nap time: "You took a good nap. I bet you feel rested." If you've been doing your work and your child wants to play, you might say, "I need to finish what I'm doing first. I'll set the timer to remind me to stop in 15 minutes. Then you and I can play a game you pick for 15 minutes so you'll get a turn to play. When the timer goes off, I'll have to go back to my work. You can keep playing, or you can watch one TV show we agree on."

After Dinner: "Tonight you need to take a bath. After you're all dried off and have your pajamas on, we'll straighten up the bathroom together. Then after you brush your teeth, I'll read a story, and then it will be bedtime."

Avoid getting trapped by all of the usual arguments.

"But I don't want to."

"You don't have to *want to*. You just *have to*."

Then start filling the bathtub.

6

Helping Kids Learn Self-Control

6-11 Years

By the time our children reach school age, most of us have long since given up the hope of raising perfect children. In fact, most of us have done or said a few of those things that we vowed we would *never* do or say. Kids have a way of testing us and humbling us. This testing and humbling can become a game, a competition of wills. One of the results of playing this game and losing is "The G.A.S. Trap." Without knowing why or how they're doing it, some kids learn to use *Guilt*, *Anger* and *Silence* to win at life.

THE G.A.S. TRAP

G-guilt (Stage 1)

A-anger (Stage 2)

S-silence (Stage 3)

The G.A.S. trap usually moves in sequence from Stage 1 to Stage 3, and it's been my experience that the trap gets tighter as you move from stage to stage. On occasion a kid will skip guilt and start with anger or silence, but you still feel guilty. The goal in any case is to avoid getting trapped.

THE GUILT TRIP

Children are great organizers of guilt trips, so Stage 1 often begins like this: "Mom/Dad, if you won't let me do such and such activity or buy me this or that, all of the other kids will make fun of me, and I'll be the only one left out. So please, p-l-e-a-s-e!?" As soon as you start feeling just the least bit guilty and thinking that maybe you aren't such a good parent after all, you have begun the guilt trip.

Many of us have been conditioned to try to give our kids whatever they ask for. Parents who are conditioned like this have difficulty seeing the difference between wants and needs. I heard one man quote Matthew 7:9-11 as his reason for trying to fulfill all requests:

> Which of you, if his son asks for bread, will give him a stone? Or if he asks for a fish, will give him a snake? If you, then, though you are evil, know how to give good gifts to your children, how much more will your father in heaven give good gifts to those who ask him!

Stop and think for a moment—has God given you everything you've asked for? Has he asked you to wait for some things? Has he said "no" to others? Isn't it all right then to say "no" to your kids and not feel guilty about it? Say something like, "Well, I know it's no fun to be left out, but I just don't think what you're asking for is a good idea, so I'm going to say 'no.'"

FITS OF ANGER

After a few more attempts to get you to bite down on the guilt bait, they'll proceed to Stage 2, *Anger.* "I can't stand you! All the other kids say I have the meanest parents, and I tried to stand up for you, but now I know they're right. I hate you!"

Anger is a very natural emotion. When it is used to express the feelings of the moment, then it's a legitimate way to share our hurt and frustration. Anger is like a smoke detector that warns us we have a problem. The anger says loud and clear that something has caused hurt or frustration. When anger is used to attack, however, it becomes a weapon, and its design is to get someone to change his mind.

When your child uses an anger attack, say something like, "Sorry you feel that way, but if you change your mind, please let me know." About this time he'll storm off down the hall, loudly slamming the door to his room for emphasis, just in case you didn't get the message that he's mad. He wants to control!

THE SILENT TREATMENT

Stage 3, *Silence*, starts as the parent goes down the hall after their kid, quietly knocking on the door lest he upset this frail bundle of nerves any further, and says, "Hon, can we talk? Hon, are you in there? Now don't be mad. (That was his intent, remember?) Can we talk? (Don't hold your breath.)" Then the parent opens the door a crack and peers timidly in. The youngster is on the bed, music blasting, eyes teared, mouth closed and, whether the parent knows it or not, ears tuned into another world. They'll build igloos in Miami before that iceberg melts, so leave it alone for a while. Time and warmth always melt ice.

Next time your kid storms off down the hall, consider it a good omen because then you'll have about two hours to read a book, watch what you want on TV, take a hot bath or even take a nap. So enjoy your time. Besides, no fish ever got caught but what bit the bait. Recognize

G.A.S. traps for what they are, guilt-loaded tricks that all kids learn to use while still quite young. If they didn't use G.A.S. from time to time, then folks like me would probably wonder what was wrong with the kid. So cancel out the guilt trip. Your child may offer you the tickets, but you don't have to go along for the ride.

When a child says, "I hate you," avoid the temptation to say, "Oh, no, you don't!" All people, even grade school children, have intense emotional experiences at times. To tell a child, "You don't feel that way" either denies the child's experience or says you can't handle a tense situation, neither of which you want to convey. It's one thing to joke when a kid's giving you G.A.S., but when the emotion is real, then sit down and talk about, "What is it about me that you hate?" If you're willing to keep the conversation going without getting defensive, you'll probably have a very productive talk.

If your child gets angry and says, "You're the meanest mom in the world!" shrug your shoulders and say, "Thanks, I've always wanted to be famous for something. I guess that makes you famous, too! Now, what's the real problem?"

G.A.S. AND THE STEPPARENT

Stepchildren may be more adept at pumping G.A.S. than most. On weekend visits stepparents are hit with statements like, "You're not my *real* mother. I don't have to do that when I'm at my *real* home." The best response for this is something like, "You're ever so right. I know I'm not your *real* mother, but I am your *real* father's *real* wife, so do what I said *real* quick." If both natural parents are around, children have to learn to live in two different homes. Sometimes parents will use the kids as weapons to get back at their ex. Stepchildren will take advantage of this situation by using the casket-like G.A.S. trap. It'll seem like there's no way out alive.

Stepchildren are quick to point out the variation in rules between their two households, "But that's not the rule at my real mother's house."

"That's fine, George. When you're at your real mother's house we expect you to go by her rules, and when you're at our house, we expect you to go by our rules. I know that's tough, but I know you can handle it without any problem."

Stepparents play a special role in a child's life, yet there is no possible way they can ever be fully prepared for the stepparenting experience. Your spouse's children from a previous marriage will always be a part of your present marriage in some fashion. The sooner you accept that fact the better for all concerned.

An excellent resource for stepfamilies is the book *The Boys and Girls Book About Stepfamilies* by Dr. Richard Gardner (available in paperback from Creative Therapeutics, P. O. Box R, Cresskill, N.J. 07626-0317, $3.50 plus $2 postage and handling). If you have stepchildren, I recommend this book.

Chart 4 on the next page suggests that during grade school years children are capable of more personal decisions. The experiences of these years provide children the opportunity to be responsible for their schedules, homework, rooms and friends. These responsibilities involve major decisions, and that's the way it should be.

THREE CRITICAL LESSONS

During your child's first three school years, each day is a new experiment in the laboratory of life. At school the kids learn basics like readin', 'ritin' and 'rithmetic — the three R's of education. At home the curriculum is more

Common Sense Discipline Chart 4

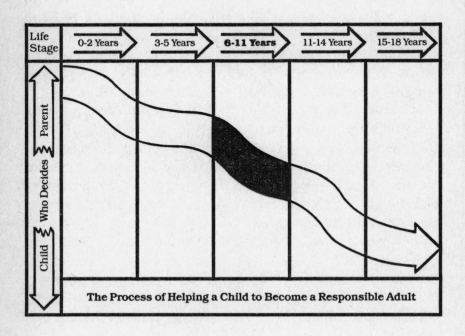

| Life Stage | 0-2 Years → | 3-5 Years → | **6-11 Years** → | 11-14 Years → | 15-18 Years → |

The Process of Helping a Child to Become a Responsible Adult

(Vertical axis labeled: Who Decides — Parent / Child)

practical. Parents are the teachers of how to grow up — the three R's of life: reliability, resourcefulness and responsibility. These "grown-up" qualities take years to develop, but they must take root during the grade school years.

Reliable

A reliable child will learn to complete chores and follow instructions on his own. Rules and limits help him to know what to do and when to do it. Schedules and daily routines help him organize activities so he remembers and completes them on his own.

Resourceful

Some children seem to be born resourceful while others appear at times to have all the lights on, but nobody's home. A resourceful child will take charge of his own life and solve problems as they arise. No longer is there a need for constant adult supervision. In fact, a resourceful youngster likes to be free to develop his own interests and work on them on his own.

Responsible

Children are not genetically programmed to be responsible — they need training! A responsible child takes care of his room, his clothes, his possessions and himself (although not necessarily in that order). He begins to enjoy caring for others too. Each day he seems to be more and more aware that he is programmed for independence.

SUZY AND THE THREE R'S

The mother of a fourth grader came to my office deeply troubled. It seems that sweet little Suzy refused to take a bath unless Mom ran the water for her. Then Suzy would complain until Mom scrubbed her back. Suzy wouldn't get dressed unless Mom laid out her clothes. Of course, Mom's selections were never the right ones. Suzy's responsibility program seemed to be on hold, resourcefulness was questionable, and reliability was out to lunch. Mom was at the end of her frazzled rope. Our conversation went like this:

"What can I do? She refuses to take a bath unless I scrub her back, and then she won't go to school unless I take her in the car."

"How far is it to the school?" I asked.

"Four blocks."

"How do the other kids in your neighborhood get to school?"

"They walk or ride their bikes."

"What would happen if you let Suzy get to school on her own?"

"She'd probably be late, because she waits until the very last minute because she knows I'll have to take her."

"Have to take her?" I said incredulously.

"Well, if I didn't, she'd be tardy because she waits so long."

"Uh huh. And then what would happen if she came to school tardy?"

"Well, I guess she'd get a detention and have to stay after school."

"Uh huh, and how long do you think Suzy would allow that to happen before she decided to get going on time to avoid being tardy again?"

"OK, I think I see what you mean. Well, I could let her be tardy, but still she'd wear the most outlandish clothes if I didn't select some for her."

"I know that's embarrassing, but if the clothes were really inappropriate, what would her teachers do?"

"They'd probably send her home and make her serve a detention for the classes she missed."

"OK, what do you think would happen if you quit cooperating with her stalling routine and stopped drawing her bath and scrubbing her back? They don't even give that kind of service in expensive hotels, so why do you do it at home?"

"Well, if I didn't make her take a bath, she'd probably go to school smelling bad."

"Uh huh, and how long do you think it would be before the other kids or teachers said something to her about it?"

"Oh, OK. In other words, you think she's old enough to learn to take care of this by herself, or suffer the consequences?"

"Right. If she's smart enough to figure out how to manipulate you, the adult who's supposed to be in charge here, then she's certainly smart enough to figure out how to be responsible, resourceful and self-reliant."

DEVELOPING A PLAN

Don't let a few disappointments destroy your confidence as a parent. Your child didn't learn to walk without falling down, and he won't grow up without messing up. Hebrews 10:32-36 sounds like it was written just to help parents hold on to their confidence.

Remember those earlier days after you had received the light, when you stood your ground in a great contest in the face of suffering. Sometimes you were publicly exposed to insult and persecution; at other times you stood side by side with those who were so treated. You sympathized with those in prison and joyfully accepted the confiscation of your property, because you knew that you yourselves had better and lasting possessions.

So do not throw away your confidence; it will be richly rewarded. You need to persevere so that when you have done the will of God you will receive what he has promised.

Learning to be reliable, resourceful and responsible takes years of living. Don't expect these lessons to be learned without your share of difficult times. Although there are no magic potions that will guarantee success, you will discover a deep reservoir of self-confidence if you have a plan. Turning your home into a laboratory of life demands some kind of lesson plan. It is God's will that you "Train a child in the way he should go" (Proverbs 22:6), and all training requires a plan of action.

A successful plan of action will help your child develop reliability, resourcefulness and responsibility while you are becoming more self-confident. As a bare minimum, your plan must have these seven steps:

1. Talk It Out
2. Get Inside Their Heads
3. Make the Rules
4. Break It Down
5. Show Them How
6. What Will Happen
7. Did It Work?

Developing your plan will also rescue you from the G.A.S. trap!

Talk It Out

The first step in helping your child to develop the reliability, resourcefulness and responsibility that Suzy didn't have is spending time talking with child. Talking gives you the opportunity to (1) get to know what he is thinking and feeling, (2) set and discuss appropriate rules of behavior and (3) share your expectations.

Get Inside Their Heads

At times asking questions is the only way to get information. Some kids will never voluntarily tell you anything about what's going on inside their heads. Try a family interview night. It can be fun, interesting and very informative. Use questions like:

☐ Who is your favorite teacher?

☐ If you could have any wish granted, what would it be?

☐ What sport do you enjoy the most?

☐ Who is your greatest hero?

☐ How do you know God is listening to your prayers?

☐ What embarrasses you the most?

☐ Who is your best friend?

☐ What really makes you angry?

☐ What is the best gift you have ever received?

☐ What do you think God does all day?

☐ What is your favorite song?

☐ How do you act when you are really angry?

☐ Where would you like to go for vacation?

☐ What is your biggest fear?

☐ What is something you are good at?

☐ What kind of job do you want to have when you grow up?

☐ Tell me what you think heaven will be like.

☐ How do you like doing these interviews?

Make the Rules

Every family has rules. Every family needs rules. Tell the following story, and ask your child to make up his own ending.

> Once there was a king in a small country who was very unhappy. He had to listen to all the cases where the people broke the law. This kept him very busy all day long, so he got very tired of all the people breaking the law. One day he thought, "I wonder what it would be like if there were no laws? If there are no laws then there would be no

lawbreakers, and I would have no cases to listen to all day." So he decreed that beginning tomorrow people could do anything they want to. There would be no more law. The next day...

This story will help you discuss the need for rules. The bottom line is that rules only work if the children know what the rules are. Get the kids together and make a list of the rules in your family. You will find that you probably have rules on the following subjects:

bedtime	homework
toys	television
food	play
clothes	work
speech	friends

Rules should be simple and positive. They are meant to help people, not hurt people. After you have brainstormed your list of rules, vote on the 10 most important ones.

Discussions like this help your children to see the need for the rules your family has adopted. Then as you make more rules about behavior, the kids will have an easier time accepting the rules without getting "exasperated" (Ephesians 6:24). When rules are discussed they tend to be remembered, and you may even hear your kids say, "That's the way we do it at our house!" instead of "That's the dumb rule my parents made up!"

Break It Down

Learning to be responsible does not happen in one "super lesson." Responsibility is developed bit by bit. Don't give room all at once. A job that's big must be learned a little at a time. If you want your child to keep his room neat, first let him have responsibility for taking his dirty clothes to the laundry room. Then later he can work on vacuuming, dusting and washing woodwork.

Charts help children develop reliability, resourcefulness and responsibility in an organized way. There are three basic types of charts that can be used:

Assignment Chart

	MORNING	EVENING
SUSAN	GAME ROOM	ASSISTANT COOK
ERIC	FAMILY ROOM	SET TABLE
TIM	BATHROOM	EMPTY DISHWASHER
JULIE	FRONT ROOM	TRASH

This chart names household tasks and helps children remember who does each job.

Fun Charts

DECORATE THE TREE

AN APPLE FOR EACH BOOK.

PICK A JOB

You can use these charts creatively to help the child discover the enjoyment and satisfaction of work.

Incentive Charts

NAMES	DATE	DATE	DATE	DATE	DATE	DATE
SUSAN	★					
ERIC			★		★	
TIM				★		
JULIE		★				★

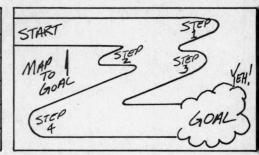

These charts use checks, stars, or stickers to show the child's accomplishment and progress.

Using charts positively can help your child to grow up. Charts work for these five reasons:

☐ Charts help us learn a task a step at a time.

☐ Charts put some excitement in the routine.

☐ They foster a sense of fairness—the child knows exactly what is expected; there are no surprises.

☐ Charts help children to think in an orderly fashion.

☐ Charts can become a source of incentive to complete the task at hand.

Show Them How

Teaching your youngster how to do something new is one of the most meaningful things a parent can do, and it is a powerful way to build your child's self-esteem. You are the most significant teacher your children will ever have. Think of all the things your youngster has learned from you: talking, walking, eating, dressing, throwing, hugging, building, cooking, trusting and fishing, just to name a few. Let me tell you about fishing.

It was six o'clock Saturday morning when Ryan was awakened by Dad's familiar voice, "Ryan, it's time to get ready!" Ryan jumped to his feet, ran to the bathroom, put on his clothes and scurried into the kitchen holding his Kangaroos (tennis shoes).

Dad looked at his watch, "Two minutes, that's a record! Are you ready to catch a record trout?"

"Yes, you bet I am. Where's my pole?" Ryan said after tying his last shoe lace.

"I put everything in the trunk," Dad said. "Let's go! First stop, McDonald's."

After a quick breakfast, the two adventurers drove to the river, parked the car and began getting ready for the hike down to the river.

"Remember," Dad said, "you need to stay close by me while we're at the river. Here's your pole, and here's mine. Do you still know how to use the reel?"

"Uh huh, but show me again."

Dad stood behind Ryan putting his hand on his son's seven-year-old inexperienced hand and demonstrated the casting and the reeling.

"I think you're ready. Show me you can do it by yourself."

Dad knew he could, and Ryan did. After reeling in the line, they headed down the mountain to the river. It was going to be the best day ever.

They fished for three hours and didn't catch a fish. Ryan followed Dad everywhere. He only tangled his line twelve times, he fell in the water twice, lost his cap and cut his knee, but he had learned to cast! A slightly disappointed and tired boy followed his dad up the trail to the car. He put his pole in the trunk without a word and climbed into the front seat.

As they drove off, Dad said, "I hope you're not too disappointed that we didn't catch any trout."

Ryan reached over, hugged Dad's leg and said, "It's OK, Dad. We'll get the trout next time."

Before Ryan drifted off to sleep, Dad asked, "What was the best part of the trip?"

Ryan barely managed to open his eyes, but without hesitation he replied, "The best part was doing what you did, except when I fell in. It was the best day evvvvvv...."

Dad grinned and locked those words away forever.

Make sure you take the time to show your child how to do a task before you discipline the child for not doing it. Sometimes we forget.

WHAT WILL HAPPEN

Just as it's important for our children to be shown how to do a required task, it is also important that they know exactly what will happen if they don't do it. I have already dealt with the basics of establishing consequences for misbehavior; now let me fine tune a bit.

Imagine two sisters washing the dishes after dinner. This particular evening they are arguing between themselves concerning who is supposed to load the dishwasher and who is supposed to clean up the kitchen.

As the girls get louder and louder, Mom finally is fed up, "Since you girls are having so much trouble with this task, you can spend the evening washing every dish in the cabinet. Start now!"

Wow, how about overkill! This kind of consequence will breed resentment and bitterness.

Let's try it again...As the girls get louder and louder, Mom finally is fed up, "Since you girls are having trouble with this task, you can take turns doing it alone. Tonight will be Julie's turn. Start now!"

By the way, if you make an overkill consequence in anger or out of a misunderstanding, correct it right then. Tell the child how you feel, and adjust the consequence as you see fit. You may be able to save yourself from a load of guilt. Good consequences build acceptance, while bad consequences build resentment and rejection. Living with the results of our actions is part of growing up. These consequences keep the outside in line while our child is developing reliability, resourcefulness and responsibility on the inside.

All kinds of incentives can encourage grown-up behavior. Parents could use any or all of the following as incentives or rewards:

- Verbal strokes
- Personal notes
- Special certificates
- Privileges
- Favorite foods
- A challenge or bet
- Money
- Even an unexpected reaction, like laughing or joking, can be an incentive.

Did It Work?

Every plan needs constant evaluation. One early morning conversation may lead you to a deeper level of confidence in your child's reliability, or watching your young-

ster play with a friend may show you a resourcefulness you
have never seen before. Noticing your child outgrowing the
charts may help you sense the new level of responsibility
now present in him. This new information will require you
to modify your plan of action, and that's good.

Sometimes evaluation results in recognizing that it's
not working. This requires a different kind of change. For
example, it is rather normal to find a little procrastination
in all of our children. Some, however, have developed the
habit of procrastinating. To deal effectively with this problem, you should ask three questions:

1. How can you tell if your child is a procrastinator?
   Look for:

   ☐ Delays in starting tasks

   ☐ Slowness in finishing task

   ☐ Excuse making

   ☐ Consistently messy work

   ☐ Continual waiting for help

   ☐ Expressions of boredom

   ☐ Staying away when there's work to do

2. What could be the reason? Consider:

   ☐ Fear of failure

   ☐ Expectation of perfection

   ☐ Overwhelming task

   ☐ Non-challenging task

   ☐ Addiction to TV

   ☐ Ignorance about the task

   ☐ A pattern of uncompleted tasks

3. What are my options? Try:

- ☐ Praising positive efforts however small they may be
- ☐ Offering something new and different in the process
- ☐ Adjusting the task to fit the child
- ☐ Insisting on keeping at it until finished
- ☐ Using charts to help build a pattern of success
- ☐ Appealing to a sense of competition
- ☐ Helping them to develop necessary skills

ARE YOUR EXPECTATIONS REALISTIC?

Although it seems complicated, helping kids learn to be reliable, resourceful and responsible comes naturally — if we'll let it. Letting our children experience the consequences of their behavior will teach lessons that lectures will never touch.

Don't expect to develop a plan that works great the first time. Plans are good only if they are realistic, and sometimes it takes a little experience to get realistic. You should know your child better than anyone else, so trust your instincts and lean on the Lord.

Remember, the goal is to raise children who learn how to be responsible adults — they aren't adults yet!

7

Solutions That Make Sense

6-11 Years

Even with the best of intentions and the best plan of action, problems still poke holes in our confidence. We desperately want to do right, but as Lewis Carroll suggests, we have to have a problem (do something wrong) before we can learn the solution (do what is right).

> **Alice:** Where I come from, people study what they are NOT good at in order to be able to do what they ARE good at. Grown-ups tell us to find out what we did wrong and never do it again.
>
> **Mad Hatter:** That's odd! It seems to me that in order to find out about something, you have to study it. And when you study it, you should become better at it. Why would you want to become better at something and then never do it again?
>
> **Alice:** Nobody ever tells us to study the right things we do. We're only supposed to learn from the wrong things. But, we are permitted to study the right things other people do. And sometimes we're even told to copy them.

Mad Hatter: That's cheating!

Alice: You're quite right, Mr. Hatter. I do live in a topsy-turvy world. It seems like I have to do something wrong first in order to learn from that what not to do. And then, by not doing what I'm not supposed to do, perhaps I'll be right. But I'd rather be right the first time, wouldn't you?

Lewis Carroll, *Through the Looking Glass*

Although Alice would like to do things right the first time, she really does learn more by what she does wrong. When we face problems in our family, it's usually because someone has done something wrong. Pointing out what's wrong, however, will not solve the problem. To solve our problems we must make sure we know exactly what went wrong. We must learn from our mistakes what not to do. Then we must concentrate on the right things we do to solve the problem.

In other words, we can spend our time worrying about what went wrong, or we can knuckle down and figure out what right things we can do to fix it.

This chapter is filled with typical childhood problems that need no-nonsense solutions. Look for the solutions that are right for you.

EARLY MORNING TENSIONS

The five minutes just before leaving for school has traditionally become the loudest five minutes in America. For decades, mothers from coast to coast have been recorded yelling these things:

- ☐ "Hurry up! You're going to be late!"
- ☐ "Did you brush your teeth?"
- ☐ "Can't you leave each other alone?"

☐ "You'd forget your head if it wasn't attached!"

☐ "Eat your lunch today. Don't trade it away!"

☐ "Come straight home — no goofing off!"

To solve the early morning tension time, divide the morning routine into specific tasks and help your youngster to become responsible for each task one at a time. At the right time you might find it helpful to tell your child: "When the school bus/car pool comes, I expect you to be ready. If you aren't, then I'll put the rest of your clothes in a paper bag and toss them in the bus. You will have to finish dressing on the way to school. It's your choice."

You may have to toss the bag on the bus once, but you'll never have to do it twice. If you have doubts about your child's readiness for this action, think about how old he was when he could remember the days, times and channels of his favorite TV shows.

Should the problem continue, try this: "If you are late and miss your ride and I have to take you, it will cost you. For every minute you rob from me, it will cost you five minutes of play time/TV time, starting this afternoon. So if you inconvenience me fifteen minutes, it's going to cost you 5x15 or seventy-five minutes. You decide if you want to be ready or not."

HAGGLING WITH HOMEWORK

Some parents gripe and nag at their kids, and the homework still doesn't get done. Others end up doing the homework for the child. Either way, the child does not learn to be responsible for his own assignments. Even though the child has his own desk, his own computer and

his own encyclopedias, he may not have his own self-dis-
cipline. He may be just plain lazy.

Some children need additional incentives to encourage
them to study harder and make good grades. If your child
is doing poorly in school mainly because of laziness, try
this:

1. Stop all nagging about study. Prepare yourself and
   your child for a change. This will put his grades
   squarely on his own back.
2. Provide some special incentives to make study
   worthwhile. You might say, "Look, it's important to
   me that you make better grades. I know it may be
   hard to do that, but I'm willing to make it worth
   your while. For each passing grade you bring home
   from now on, here's what you will get:

	GOOD GRADE CHART		
GRADE	DAILY ASSIGNMENTS	WEEKLY TESTS	COURSE GRADES
A	3 points	9 points	$3
B	2 points	6 points	$2
C	1 point	3 points	$1

"In addition to the points you receive for grades, I'll
give you five points for each half hour you study at
home."

3. Before TV can be watched after school, the youngster must study 30-90 minutes each might (parent's
   choice, depending on each child's situation and
   needs).
4. Decide on a set time and place for study each day.
   Let your child pick the best time and place for him;

remember no TV until the study time is up. To earn the points, the parent must see the child studying or see the results of his work.

5. The points earned in this incentive program can be saved and traded for special activities like trips, events or appropriate surprises. What would your child pick?

RESISTANCE TO READING

Each of the ideas suggested below can kindle or rekindle your child's interest in reading.

- Collect brochures and booklets about your town. Suggest your child read the collection and make a list of the most interesting things in your city.
- Watch the TV news and discuss the people and events that made news that day. Encourage your child to read a newspaper and/or magazine article about people or events in the news.
- Ask your child to read *TV Guide* and look up the unfamiliar words.
- Ask your child to select a magazine or newspaper story. Now comes the fun. Have your child search for the longest word in the story, the grossest word and the most exciting word.
- When picking a library book, ask your child to read one page aloud and hold up one finger for every word he can't pronounce. After reading the page aloud, if five fingers are held up, the book is probably too hard — it will frustrate the child.

- Take books on vacations. Books help fill free time in cars, at campsites and in motel rooms.
- Read aloud to your kids even though they can read for themselves. The kids will enjoy the closeness and security of your voice.

Remember, the most effective way to encourage your child to read is to read. Avid readers tend to raise children who become avid readers.

FEARS AND FAILURES

Children, because of their limited knowledge of the world around them, have many kinds of fears. Some have one or two, and some collect dozens of them.

Secret fears

One eight-year-old told me the vivid story of his secret fear. It seems that each night at bedtime he would reluctantly crawl into bed praying that God would help him sleep through the night. He was comforted by having his four-year-old brother in the bed with him. Of course, the bedroom door was left wide open, and the bathroom light was always left on.

One night during a storm, his home suffered a temporary power failure. All the lights went out, including that precious bathroom light. It was as if he was awakened by the darkness. He stared intently into the lightless hallway. Strange noises and unfamiliar shadows filled his imagination to overflowing.

Suddenly a seven-foot-tall cowboy appeared. He began slowly walking toward the youngster's bed. The boy was frozen with fear. This cowboy was dressed in full cowboy-type garb: ten gallon hat, chaps, boots and twin six guns. The eight-year-old could see all these details in a pitch dark room. By the time the cowboy reached the bedside, the boy was sweating with fear. He could see the zombie-like eyes of the intruder.

Finally the boy got the courage to yell as loud as he could, "Don't kill me! No!" The cowboy continued to stare at the boy until Mom entered the room and poof! He was gone.

The active imagination of an eight-year-old painted the details of shadows and produced a vivid experience that initiated a fear, not of cowboys, but of waking up in the middle of the night.

There are many grade school children who are afraid of spiders, dogs, snakes, bees and sharks. Lots of kids are afraid to swim where fish are — they might bite them. Some are afraid of war and nuclear attack. I have counseled with children who are scared to death that their parents might get a divorce and with children who have a morbid fear of their parents dying. Kids have lots of fears.

The Fear of Trying

The fear that hurts the most is the fear of trying. Some children today are so terrified by failure that they do everything within their power not to try new things. Children with this problem find it difficult to believe in themselves. They become increasingly more dependent upon parents and other adults.

A child will be eager to try new things only as long as his feet are firmly set on the threshold of his own home. The self-confidence needed to try new things is produced at home. There are four distinct ways to encourage this self-confidence.

1. Acceptance of Failure — "I want you to know that you can never mess up badly enough for me to stop

loving you. Whether you become a president or a prisoner, I will always love you!"

2. Social Security—"You are a special part of this family; you belong here. Everybody has to belong somewhere, and you belong here!"

3. Repeat Successes — "I believe you are best at . . . I like to watch people do their best, so would you do it for me? Thank you, I love it!"

4. Assign Responsibility—"This is your task. Here is how you do it. Practice it. Once you can do it by yourself, it will be your responsibility in this family. If you don't do it, it won't get done!"

Failing in School

About a month before school let out for the summer, a mother came to my office with her fifth grade son. She was distraught because it appeared he might fail. He wasn't doing his homework at all.

"What's wrong with allowing him to fail? Sounds to me like he wants to fail. Can't he make it up in summer school?"

"Yes, but we've planned a special trip to Mexico this summer, and the tickets have already been purchased. If we cancel our reservations now, there will be a sizable penalty. It's our first vacation in years. I thought we were all looking forward to the trip."

We developed a plan of action, and this is what I told her son: "Billy, I understand you may fail the fifth grade. If you do, you'll need to repeat the grade in summer school. As you know, your folks have been worried sick (loaded with guilt) because they feel they'll have to cancel their vacation plans because of your summer school. We've worked out a way for your parents and sister to still get to go on their trip, though you may miss out." Now we had his attention.

"Your mom and I discussed making arrangements with Mrs. Jones who lives down the street from you. You'll stay at her house while your folks are gone, and Mrs. Jones will take you to summer school. Mom and Dad will pay her room and board for your expenses in advance. Of course, due to the extra expense you'll have to do extra work at your house and Mrs. Jones' house during the summer. Of course, if your grades come up and you pass, then you can still go on vacation with your family."

One week later at her follow-up visit, the mother said, "I don't believe it. We saw you on Thursday, and by Monday morning he had completed three major projects that were overdue. I just don't believe it!"

"You mean he cheated?" I asked.

"No, the work was all in his writing. I just don't know how he did it. He must have studied all night Friday and most of the weekend."

As it turned out, the boy passed, and the entire family enjoyed their vacation together.

Great things happen when you let children become responsible for the consequences of their own behavior.

CLOTHES, CLOSETS AND COOPERATION

You may find your grade schooler going through several changes of clothes in a day. If he puts his clothes in the proper places, it wouldn't be such a problem, but since the parent usually does the laundry, then we have a problem.

To encourage your child to put his clothes back in the closet or in the proper place, this rule may help: Before you can watch TV or play during the evening, you must straighten up your room by putting away all clothes in their proper places.

Ideas for Clothes Care

- Look at the closet from the child's eye level. Use bright padded hangers (kids like them). Install clothes hooks in the closet. Make sure the closet pole is hanging within easy reach of your child.
- Have a dirty clothes bag, basket or box in the child's room. Perhaps you might have two: one for light colored clothes and the other for dark colors.
- Use plastic stacking bins for clothes organizers.
- Show your child how to use the washing machine.
- Have your child use a nylon or mesh laundry bag for socks — just toss the whole bag in the washer and dryer. He will be able to sort them himself.
- Before bedtime have your child lay out clothes for the next day, including shoes. (There is more time to find lost shoes at night than just before school.)

Scattered Clothes

If your children enter the house doing a "strip act," dropping a coat here, a soccer shirt there and school books in the kitchen, then it's time for action. Say: "If I have to pick up these things of yours, it will cost you! The price is five minutes of play time or TV time for each thing of yours. I want you to learn to remember."

TV: ADOPTED OR ADAPTED

The following suggestions are proven ways to adapt TV for positive use in your home.

- Carefully select the shows your family watches and insist that certain shows are off-limits.
- Set aside a time for family shows that you watch as a family. When parents and children express their views about a program, everyone gains insights about the program and each other.
- Include the children in decisions about what you will watch during the week. Select a special time each week when the TV log will be reviewed and marked for the week.
- Don't use the TV as a baby-sitter. There is more problem with what TV keeps us from doing as a family than with what it does to a family.
- Ask your child to think of another title for the program or series you are watching. Vote on the best suggestion.
- Have your child write a description or review of the program after viewing it. Keep these reviews to use in selecting favorite TV shows of the year for your family.
- During a commercial break ask: "What will happen next?"
- Ask your child to time the commercials during a show and give you the total at the end of the show.
- Have your child draw a picture describing his feelings about a show; then discuss the picture.
- Turn off the volume but leave the picture on. Ask your children to make up some funny new dialogue for the action on the screen.

Without placing limits on the use of TV in your family, you may find yourself adopting TV as a member of your family — that would be tragic.

WHEN MEANNESS HURTS

Children learn how powerful words are by what happens when they use them. If a word like "stupid" gets people's attention, then children will say "stupid" when they want attention. The tragedy is that while words like "stupid," "dumb," "dork" and "geek" get attention, they also can do great damage.

These simple little words used in the wrong setting can destroy even the healthiest self-esteem. It does little good to pretend we're immune to the pain. No one likes being put down by others. Grade school children are the most vulnerable of all.

The old children's verse should read like this:

> "Sticks and stones may break my bones,
> But names will never hurt me;
> They just bruise my heart."

If parents and teachers will follow this four-step plan, they can help their kids handle the cruel put-downs, jokes and names that inevitably come.

Step 1 — Intervene.

After thirty minutes of staring in the mirror, wishing the new glasses would disappear, Ronnie approached Mom one more time.

"Mom, do I have to wear these glasses today? None of the other first graders have to wear glasses!"

"Yes! You look fine, and I know you can see better. So just think about how much better you can see. Come on, it's time for school."

Ronnie whispered to that still worried little boy in the mirror, "I don't think you look fine!"

Ronnie picked up his lunch and hurried out the door. For a moment he forgot his worry. He made a startling discovery; there was a wire stretched between those telephone poles. Now, he knew how the birds were able to just sit there in the air. He really could see a lot better.

Wouldn't you know it, as soon as he walked on the school yard, Wayne, the meanest boy at school yelled, "Hey, look at four eyes. He's got some dumb new glasses!"

Ronnie ran as fast as he could, but not fast enough to stop the tears. He got to his first grade classroom as the bell was ringing. As he wiped the tears from his eyes, Mrs. Smith, his teacher, told him how much she liked his new glasses. Phil, his best friend, wanted to try them on, but Ronnie didn't pay any attention. All Ronnie could hear was "Four eyes! Four eyes!"

At lunch time Wayne was standing by the drinking fountain when Ronnie rounded the corner. Wayne yelled, "Hey, four eyes, what's the matter, are you blind?" While Wayne was yelling, Mrs. Smith came around the corner. She heard the harrassment and said, "Boys, come over here, right now. Ronnie, you too."

Ronnie was scared to death. He hadn't done anything.

Mrs. Smith stooped down, looked straight at Wayne and said, "Wayne, we do not make fun of people around here. We think everyone is special, but we know no one is perfect. To make fun of Ronnie's glasses is mean and hateful, and I want you to stop. Now! Do you understand?"

Wayne looked off in the distance, but he said he understood.

"OK, go on and play," she said.

That incident didn't stop Wayne from calling Ronnie names, but it helped change Ronnie's attitude. Mrs. Smith made him feel special. By challenging Wayne she helped Ronnie to feel more sure of himself and his glasses.

We must be ready to intervene in whatever way seems appropriate.

Step 2 — Listen.

While Mom was visiting with Grandma, Carrie ran ahead to the playground. When she arrived, her friend Heather was sitting on a bench by the swings. The boys on the swings were calling her names and proudly chanting, "Girls are dumb! We hate girls!"

Carrie ran up and helped Heather.

Later, Carrie's mother and grandma arrived. When Carrie saw her mom, she grabbed Heather's hand and ran to her mom's bench. "Mom, Mom," Carrie cried. "See those boys over there? They were yelling at Heather and calling her names so I helped her."

Mom asked, "What did you help her do?"

"I helped her cry!" Carrie said as the girls walked off arm in arm.

Carrie's mom learned a lesson that day. Later she wrote in her diary: "...It seems that my first inclination would have been to defend and rescue, but after watching Heather and Carrie, I think rescue may not be as healing as sharing the hurt."

The Bible suggests a very simple formula for helping people. "Be happy with those who are happy. Be sad with those who are sad" (Romans 12:15, NCV). Empathy, feeling what your child is feeling, opens the door for healing.

Step 3—Tell when something similar happened to you.

Your kids love to hear stories about when you were their age. Share how you felt when kids called you names. Tell all the details. Include what you did and what you learned.

There will be times when you will find it helpful to tell about a time when you were guilty of name calling. Sharing these stories helps kids cope.

Step 4 — Encourage your child to do something kind.

Doing something kind for another child helps to relieve the sting of being put down. Kindness helps get the focus off the offended child and onto someone else.

Kindness is best taught by practicing it. In fact, kindness is not kindness until it is acted out. This will be a great teaching moment to use later. So, remember the details.

The amazing thing about these painful times is that doing something for another child is one of the few actions that really helps. The kindness actually takes the place of the hurt.

ALLOWANCES AND MONEY MATTERS

Everyone needs an allowance. An allowance is money that can be spent any way you want. When we get to be adults, we call this our "mad money."

Giving your child an allowance is a great way to begin teaching about the value of money, the difference between "wants" and "needs" and money management skills. You will find these guidelines helpful in setting the amount of allowance:

- A fair allowance might be equal to the cost of a movie and snack per week. Some parents pro-rate the amounts given based on age. The weekly allowance might be $.50 for each year of age. A ten-year-old would get $5 weekly. If you have several kids, adjust the amount to fit your family situation.

- Check with parents of your child's friends
  to see what they are doing; then do about
  the same, if you can.

A good time to start allowances is when your child is able to keep up with lunch money at school. Try using lunch money as a "trial" allowance. Give the money at the first of the week and if your child handles the responsibility, continue the allowance. If not, try giving the money on a daily basis.

When your child begins getting an allowance, he will occasionally waste his allowance on "junk." Expect it! Rather than intervening, use the natural consequence to teach a lesson. If your child blows his money on junk, sooner or later he's bound to ask for more money to buy something important. That's your signal to say, "I really think that's something you should use your allowance for."

"But I don't have any left," comes the reply.

"Well then, you will have to wait until next week." Running out of money too early will usually take care of the junk problem if parents don't dole out extra cash.

It is important to realize that the young child will learn about money matters by trial and error. Don't expect perfection.

ERASING FOUR-LETTER WORDS

Have you wondered where kids learn to swear and use dirty language? I asked several grade schoolers and got replies like these:

- "I learned to swear when my dad was fixing the car."
- "My friend's uncle taught him, and he taught me."
- "I'm not sure."
- "I learned from school, of course."

- "I learned dirty words at the movies. My friend told me what the words meant, so I remembered them."

There seems to be a number of ways to deal with the dirty language and swearing problem. I can think of at least four:

1. Question the meaning. Say: "That's an interesting word. What does it mean? Where did you learn it?" You will get some surprising answers.
2. Use the moment for discussion. It may be that the dirty word will give you the opportunity to talk about sexuality and sex education.
3. Ask your child to tell you what he's mad at. Say, "Sometimes people use words like that when they are mad at another person. If you are angry with a person, it is better to tell him you're angry."
4. Explain and set the rules. You have the right and the obligation to set the standards for language in your house. Remind the child about the rule: No one uses words like that in this house.

ELIMINATING LYING

Lying can become a habitual problem during elementary school years unless parents take decisive action early. Children tell lies for several reasons. Sometimes they feel like they have to make up stuff for people to listen to them. Sometimes the child is just trying to protect himself from severe punishment. For example: "All right! Who got my tools out and left them in the garage all over the floor? Whoever did it is going to get his head knocked clean off!" What would you do? Some children lie for revenge and resistance.

Lying is a signal to stop and spend some quality one-on-one time with your child. Say: "You know I love you very much, but I've been noticing something that really bothers me. And I want to talk about it. It seems to me that you have been lying a lot lately. That makes me sad. The lying must stop. What can I do to help you stop?"

Remind your youngster that it will always go better for him if he tells the truth up front. He may still have to face the consequences of his actions, but lying will always make it worse.

Try these approaches for one or two weeks. Then I would urge you to get some help from a qualified therapist. Ask your physician or minister to recommend one.

BULLIES AND BANDITS

I am convinced that bullies and bandits simply test parents and teachers to see whether the adults are willing to take the lead and be in charge.

Granted, there are times when a pattern of aggression has been developed over time. One mother in a parents' meeting said, "I have an eight-year-old who is always fighting and smarting off. I can't keep my eye on him all the time. So when it gets bad, I sit on him pretty hard. It seems like the more I take charge, the more violent he gets."

The facts were that this lady and her husband got in knockdown fights all the time. We fool ourselves to think we can teach our children not to hit by hitting them.

BREAKING BAD HABITS

In order to help our children break bad habits, we apply the pressure, for instance:

Punishment—"Your room is a mess, so no friends can come over today."

Nagging—"Get ready for bed, brush your teeth, don't mess around, remember..."

Shaming—"You should be ashamed of a paper like that. I can't believe you turned in that kind of work."

Warning—"If you don't stop that kicking, I'll nail your shoes to the floor. Do you understand?"

Habits are not broken with comments like those. Try one of the following plans of action.

- Create a new, competing habit to take the place of the old undesirable one.
- Wear out the old habit — repeat it until the child is disgusted and exhausted (negative practice).
- Change the setting of the habit to unset the pattern.

ACCEPTING LIMITATIONS

Late one night I watched a B-grade movie about a mad scientist. I have forgotten the name of the flick, but the plot made a lasting impact.

The scientist and his wife were working in his laboratory late into the evening when one of the experiements backfired. The wife who was standing closest to the experiment was burned badly. Her face was char-broiled and became a frightening scab. The scientist kept her face covered so others would not look at her. He smashed all the mirrors as a kindness to her. He didn't think she could handle the rejection of others and the reality of her face.

The more he tried to protect her, the more she resented him. The hero of the flick brings her a mirror. She takes off the bandages and looks for the first time at her mangled face. She was not pretty. In fact, her skin looked like a potato, but she survived the experience. Finally she could accept herself.

Parents have to accept themselves and their limitations. Also, we must begin to accept our children and their limitations. If we have expectations that are far beyond our limitations, then we have set ourselves up for failure and continual frustration. The challenge of parenting is to let your children be all they can be by accepting themselves.

REVIEWING YOUR PERSPECTIVE

It's easy to spend all our time concentrating on problems, but that gives us an off-balanced perspective of parenthood. The plan is to use the problems to teach our kids reliability, resourcefulness and responsibility. Don't let your feelings and negative attitudes mess up your plan.

Keep your perspective on the process of *helping*. We are *helping* our kids to become responsible adults. Since we don't have a vision of the future, we are called to have faith in God. Only God can see that far ahead; that's his job. Our job is to *help* our kids learn how to live life right now.

8

Common Sense with Sensitive Ears

11-14 years

DO YOU KNOW THESE YOUNG TEENS?

It may seem like your youngster has traded personalities, or you may feel you have totally lost contact. Either way, whether you know it or not, you can bet your life there is constant activity in his head. He is putting together images of what he might be, and he is going to do it by trial and error. Look for your young teen in the following descriptions. I think you will find him in or between the lines.

Kevin's Story

Kevin had a hunch that this wasn't going to be a good day. It was Thursday, the day Mrs. Myers, his 7th grade counselor, would give him his class schedule. It was the fourth day of classes, and he didn't have a schedule yet. For three days he had been cooped up in the cafeteria taking placement tests. This just wasn't fair!

157

"Kevin! Kevin? Here's your schedule!" Mrs. Myer had interrupted one of Kevin's favorite daydreams, but he took the schedule anyway.

He glanced at the pink slip of paper and noticed that his first period class was English with Mr. Bell, and his second period was P.E. Fourth period was lunch. Well, at least the schedule wasn't impossible.

Finally, it was time for class, if he could just find it. With his notebook in one hand and his schedule in the other he wandered the halls till he found room 21.

The door was closed, giving Kevin time to worry a while. A whole fist full of "what if" questions flashed through his mind. "What if they think I'm funny looking? What if they don't like my braces. What if..."

Footsteps interrupted his questions—someone was coming. Without thinking, Kevin opened the door and looked in. As soon as Kevin walked in room 21, laughter broke out everywhere. One of the students had made a funny comment and his punch line hit at the exact moment of Kevin's entry. Without knowing the facts, Kevin assumed they were laughing at him. His "what if" worry had come true. This truly was one of his most embarrassing moments.

Looking for some relief, Kevin walked over to the teacher. When Mr. Bell saw the pink schedule card his first words were, "Oh, no! We don't have room for any more!" Inside Kevin's head those words bounced around like a racketball, "Oh, no...Oh, no...Oh, no!" There were no desks left in the room, so he sat down in the only empty chair.

While Mr. Bell went on with the class, Kevin looked more closely at his schedule. "Yuk!" he said out loud. He had just noticed that he also had Mr. Bell for math and science.

Later in P.E., he had fun playing football with a new friend. Kevin wasn't the best in any sport, but he liked them all and constantly dreamed about being the best.

At lunch Kevin watched the girls; the food was "garbage." At 3:00 p.m. the bell rang, and school was over. This had been the longest day in history. As he walked down the steps of school, he thought, "It isn't fair for my grade school friends to get to go to Helms Junior High, and I have to go to this dump." Kevin had moved during the summer. His junior high school was named Edmund Downer Junior High (that's the truth!). So far, it had truly been a downer for Kevin.

When Kevin got home Mom asked, "How was school?"

"OK," he replied.

"Did you like your teachers?"

"What teachers?"

"The ones who taught your classes."

"Which classes?"

"I don't know. Which classes do you have?"

"7th grade classes."

"Don't get smart with me young man!"

As Kevin walked away, he muttered, "There's not much chance of that at Downer!"

He went straight to his room before Mom could think of some chores for him to do. He turned on the stereo, laid down on the bed and dreamed of what Helms Junior High might have been like.

Before going to bed that night, he noticed that one of his eyes was a little lower on his face than the other. "I'm defective! No wonder those kids laughed at me today."

This was definitely not a good day.

He went to sleep worrying that all his days might turn out to be this horrible.

Keri's Story

Keri's story is told through these typical diary entries.

Dear Diary: I can't stand Melissa. She's a snob. Yesterday she said she was my best friend, and today she forgot my name when she was introducing me to this guy. Can you believe that? Mother tried to feed us liver tonight. Yuk!!!!!! Nobody ate it, not even Dad. I hate it when it's humid. It ruins my hair. Rick called tonight. He says he hates Melissa, too.

Dear Diary: Today a man spoke at church about how we should give money to relief work in Africa. I signed up to help, but only four showed up. That was really embarrassing. Our Bible class is the pits. I wouldn't say this out loud because God might be listening, but I think church is the pits, too. Shock!!! I don't think I'm a spiritual person; some people aren't, you know.

Dear Diary: Tonight the whole gang did all my favorite things. Party (Yeh!). Went to the mall!!! Pizza!!! It sure beat last weekend when I had to stay home Friday and Saturday to baby-sit Jason (Yuk). I know Jason is younger than me and I should be nice to him, but he is becoming a first-class pain! I really got Melissa today. I told her, "I can't believe you're not invited to Bev's party. I thought everybody got invited." (Ha,Ha) Wow, that got her.

Dear Diary: Today was the worst day of my life. I was so embarrassed. I hate Mr. Summers. I didn't start the note, Tom did. All I did was write, "OK" on the bottom of it. Then I passed it up the row, and Mr. Summers got it. He made Tom and me stand in class, and then he read the note out-loud to the whole class. I hate him! It's not fair!!! And it wasn't my fault!!!!

Dear Diary: Dad has threatened to take my extension phone away. Well, that just doesn't make sense, because then I'll just be on the other phone all the time. I had a record number of phone calls yesterday—47 between 3:00 p.m. and 10:00 p.m. Great!!!!

Dear Diary: I got my report card today. I can't believe Mr. Perkins gave me a 77 in art. I must have missed a few assignments. I guess I was talking a little. My whole gang got kicked out of McDonald's today. The manager had the nerve to accuse us of being too loud. How rude!!! We were just being normal. (Ha,Ha)

Dear Diary: Today my new favorite color is red. My favorite flavor of ice cream is "Cookies 'n Cream." And, I have a new favorite radio station. There may be something wrong with me. I seem to be changing a lot lately. Mom says I'm going crazy. Wrong!!!!!!

Dear Diary: I think my mom is out to get me. She is on the war path about my room. It's exactly like I want it. She called it a pig pen, I mean *really*! I think Mom just doesn't understand how different things are today. After all, she's been an adult forever.

Dear Diary: I found Kevin's locker today. I walked by it 12 times. Ann was with me when we saw him. I told her not to look at him, and she looked. I was soooooooo embarrassed!!! He is soooooooo cute. I told Mom I was in love—I'll never tell her that again. She said that I'm not old enough to know what love is. I don't think my mother has ever been in love like I am.

Did you meet your boy or girl in these descriptions? With all the pressures on the outside, it's hard to really get in touch with what's going on inside.

LIVING UNDER PRESSURE

It was Saturday at lunch, and I was sitting in a popular restaurant observing people. Two tables to my left was a fine-looking father-and-son team. The man was in his thirties, and the boy, I learned later, was eleven. Both wore polo shirts, casual slacks and the latest in fashionable running shoes. They looked alike, dressed alike and thought alike.

After the waitress brought their drinks, the boy put his chin on his hands and his elbows on the table. He looked straight at his dad and said, "I'm depressed, Dad!"

Dad responded, "I know; so am I."

They continued to talk as I left the restaurant. This real life experience reminded me of the pressure we put our kids under to be "mini" adults. We push them to grow up far before they're ready. It seems to me that childhood is vanishing before our eyes.

There is a scene in *Zorba the Greek* where Zorba watches a butterfly trying to break free of its cocoon. The struggle seemed too intense, so, with good intentions, Zorba bent down and breathed his warm moist breath on the butterfly. His breath released the butterfly. It was free, but its wings were not strong enough yet. The freed butterfly fought for several minutes and then died.

When a young teen is hurried and pressured to be an adult, he is like that butterfly. He is freed too early from childhood, and he launches too soon into adulthood. The stress of the transition forces him to become extremely self-focused and fearful of failure. This self-focus makes it difficult to be aware of the feelings and needs of others. Literally, this pressured teen becomes the center of his own universe.

He is expected to dress, act and think like an adult, so he play acts. He pretends. However, unlike the butterfly, he carries his cocoon around with him and occasionally slips back into the old familiar childish behavior.

Let us determine to reduce this pressure on our kids. Let us promise that we will not push our children to grow up before their time.

PUTTING THE PIECES TOGETHER

The young teen is constantly trying to put together his own puzzle of life. Just about the time he has one part together, he discovers he can't find the pieces for the other part. Trying to put a puzzle together when you can't locate all the pieces is pretty frustrating.

Add to this frustration a hormone clock that winds each young teen up differently, and you have a typical picture. In many ways a young teenager is like a juggler on a highwire who is trying to keep balanced and juggle all the balls in the air at the same time while his hands sometimes seem to stop listening to his head. It could be a mess. It undoubtedly is a challenge, but with some common sense, it *can* be an action-packed adventure thriller with a little danger and lots of excitement.

Chart 5 on the next page suggests that during the young teen years parents should be gradually releasing the decision-making process to the kids. Catching them doing it right and using logical consequences are extremely effective with these ages. In order to become responsible, the young teen must have opportunities to learn by facing the consequences of his behavor. Don't spend your time rescuing him.

Although many experts of the 1970's warned about the rebellious tendencies of the teenage years, we have since

Common Sense Discipline Chart 5

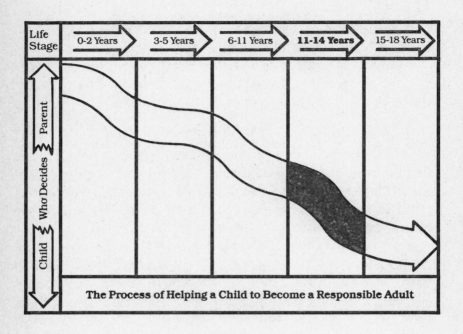

| Life Stage | 0-2 Years | 3-5 Years | 6-11 Years | **11-14 Years** | 15-18 Years |

The Process of Helping a Child to Become a Responsible Adult

discovered those warnings were based on studies of delin-quent teens. Average teens are just not bent toward rebel-lion, a little banter maybe, but not rebellion. We have good kids, and we would do well to expect the best, not the worst.

RESPONDING TO FAMOUS SAYINGS

"It's Not Fair!"

This saying needs a little interpreting. When your early teen complains that he is not being treated fairly, set up a time to have a discussion about the situation. Depending on the problem at hand, make several overdrawn, unreasonable statements like:

☐ "You can't get any new shoes because your sister's shoes are still in good shape, and I want to treat you two equally."

☐ "Since I'm feeling ill and will have to stay home, I expect you to stay home, too."

☐ "If you want to be treated equally, then I'll start buying you both exactly the same size clothes. That will make it easier to shop."

Even if they never admit it, most children will get the point. Since it's obvious they don't want to be treated equally, then you can tell them that you will do your best to treat them fairly. Fairly means you will take into account their own individual needs, differences and wants.

Let them know that whenever they feel like they are being treated unfairly, you will be willing to listen to their viewpoint so long as they are willing to listen to yours. "Is that a deal?"

Cheating. With all the pressure to perform these days, it's no wonder that young teens are cheating to make grades. Interviews with students indicate that 45-50% of young teens cheat occasionally.

● Kathy says she cheats, only a little. "You have to. The teacher grades on a curve, and about ten to twelve kids in the class cheat— they blow the curve. I've got to cheat to stay up with the class."

● Skip decided not to cheat. "I've had the chance several times to study the actual test I would take the next day, and I turned it down. I hate the way I'd feel afterwards."

● Holly added, "I don't cheat, but ratting on the kids that do is worse than cheating. It's no big deal."

We need to tighten up testing procedures. It's too easy to cheat. Look for purses with notes. Check fingernails, hands and tape on the soles and heels of shoes. Use tests that measure the integration of knowledge instead of memorized knowledge. Don't grade on the curve. We will never totally stop the cheating, but we can cut out a lot of it.

It's not fair for the majority of the students who do their own work to be hurt by the few who cheat. One school developed a "Students Against Cheating" (SAC) task force and used peer pressure to curb the cheating in the school. I like that!

Cleaning. You may find it difficult to believe, but several different surveys reveal that 65% to 75% of young teens feel they *should* be responsible for straightening and cleaning their own rooms. In addition to their own rooms, these kids should also help around the house with the regular chores. It should be that way because they are still members of the family, even though you might wonder about that at times.

It will be helpful to have a one-on-one discussion about how clean is clean. Their room is fast becoming their private world, and to challenge their world is like challenging them. Come to some kind of compromise that works for both of you. Oh yes, and pray for tolerance.

Moving. Moving your young teen at this sensitive time can be traumatic. She will feel "jerked up" from friends, school, church and her favorite mall. One or more of the following suggestions will help:

☐ Take your teenager with you when you look for your new home. Ask for her input in the selection.

☐ Have your young teen gather information about the city: schools, churches, places of special interest, recreational parks, etc.

☐ Find a teen about your teen's age to be a friend and show her the ropes.

☐ Emphasize the new start and how great it's going to be, but be willing to talk about the memories of the old place and how good it was.

☐ Encourage your teen to write friends in the old town and to keep in touch with what's happening.

"Why can't I...

...do what I want?" You can help your young teen learn responsibility by:

☐ Asking him to write a one-page proposal describing the reasons for and against doing what he wants.

☐ Trading sides in the discussion. You take your kid's side and ask him to take your side.

☐ Realizing that he may be just testing your resolve to be the leader of the family. He has developed new argument skills, and this is a great time to use them.

☐ Discussing the feelings on both sides. Listen and work out alternatives if necessary, but *never argue about feelings.*

...go where I want?" It will help your young teen to discuss the following:

☐ Ask your teen to suggest five reasons why he should get to go where he wants. You suggest five reasons why he should not. Then discuss why it's important to limit where a young teen may go.

☐ Set up some limits so that your teen knows ahead of time what places are off-limits.

☐ If you have personal experiences that relate to where your teen wants to go, share your story.

...talk like I want?" Sarcastic and critical talk is tough to deal with. Try some of these methods:

☐ Helping them to find something to do that they are good at will build their self-confidence, thus removing the motivation for being so critical. Although they are critical of others, they are most critical of themselves.

☐ Placing a moratorium on sarcastic talk for everyone in your family. *Anyone* who is critical or sarcastic has to go to time-out for five minutes.

☐ Expect a verbal apology for each sassy remark. You may not change their thinking, but you can put some limits on their talk.

☐ Doing away with all forms of put-down and sarcastic humor by anyone in your family.

"How Embarrassing!"

Keri and Her Body. When young teens are asked if they would like to change anything about their bodies, they almost always respond, "Yes!" Keri is concerned about her body. In P.E. when they have to take showers, Keri runs through the shower but hardly gets wet because she is embarrassed about her body. It seems like she's the only girl who really doesn't need a bra.

She was glad that her mother took the time to explain to her about periods and what to expect, but having her period at school is a constant source of embarrassment. She understands why some of the girls call it "The Curse."

Keri is a Christian and wants to dress modestly. Because of her convictions, there are times at the beach when she is embarrassed, but she is curious at the same time. Every once in a while, one of the gang will have a "sex" magazine. She can hardly believe what she sees on the pages. Keri's not even sure that Mom and Dad still "have sex." The whole subject is embarrassing to talk about with anyone except her close friends, so when some adult brings it up, the natural thing to do is giggle.

Keri may never ask her mom or her dad about anything related to sex. Her parents need to know what she is thinking about and what embarrasses her and what questions she has. One way to start the discussion is for one of the parents to spend some time talking about what the concerns were when he/she was a kid. These talks should be often, casual and short.

Kevin and His Body. Kevin's head is filled with concern about his body. Like Keri, he is totally embarrassed by the showers at school. He isn't nearly as developed as some of the other boys. There are times when he will spend hours wondering whether his penis will ever get to the right size or if he is defective.

During these early years of sexual development, many boys have strange fantasies about all kinds of sexual behavior. Because of these fantasies, a few boys grow up thinking they are sexually "different." Some will spend years secretly thinking that they must be homosexual because that's the only explanation they can come up with.

The first time Kevin had a wet dream he spent a week feeling guilty. Nobody had talked to him about it, and he sure wasn't going to talk to Mom or Dad. That would be total embarrassment.

While he was working on math problems at the end of math class he suddenly noticed that he had an erection. The bell rang; he put his math book in front of him and walked out of the room. That whole day he wondered if he was "oversexed" or something.

Every time Kevin masturbates he feels guilty and evil. He has never heard anyone at church talk about it, so he doesn't know what to think.

Kevin needs to talk to someone other than his peers. Most of his embarrassment is due to lack of information. For example, fears about being homosexual are fairly common today. Just because someone has weird fantasies doesn't mean he is gay. Wet dreams are a little disturbing at first, but they are natural, neither right nor wrong. Kevin's erection is what's called spontaneous erection, and most boys experience them, though not always in math class. Masturbation is practiced today by 90% of young teen boys and 50% of young teen girls. The Bible doesn't say anything about the subject, but it does talk about how problems we face can take control of us. Masturbation can become an unhealthy habit that controls a youngster early on in life.

Spend some time talking informally about your sexual struggles as a young teenager. Take regular times to talk about some of these embarrassing concerns; your teen will be glad you did, even if he never tells you so.

"I Don't Have Anything to Wear!"

Fashions and Fads. Right now the "New Wave" look is in if you are a punker. Just wait around a couple of days and something new will be the fad. In the seventh grade I once owned and actually wore a pair of blue suede shoes— can you guess why?

Kids will always have fads and fashions unique to their culture. Some will be humorous and some will be stupid. Others will take kids to the edge of acceptance by society. Often kids begin to take on the personality of the fad. When they try on more than the clothes, then it's time to discuss it, change it, or stop it.

Fitting In. One of the most difficult tasks a parent has is helping a young teenager become accepted in the group. Try some of the following ideas:

- Do some research. Find another loner who doesn't seem to fit in. Get the two together and see what happens. Remember, don't try to force friendship. The end result of force is resentment.
- Discuss friendship and the need for friends with your teen. Tell your teen that God uses our alone times to prepare us for some great service. Ask, "What do you think he is preparing you for?"
- Plan trips with families with similar-aged children.
- Realize as a parent that you can't force their friendships. Let them experience the con-

sequences of the alone time, and God will bless it. If, however, the teen seems to go into a depressed state beyond moodiness, then get some immediate counseling help.

● Pray for the right person and the right time.

"It Wasn't My Fault!"

Coping with Failure. Forgiveness is the key to coping with failure. Before a teen can pick up the pieces and learn from a failure, he must experience forgiveness. Parents can help a young teen feel forgiven only if they are willing to forgive.

However, if a child is to cope with failure, he must also face the consequences of the failure. Don't rob your teen of the consequences of his failure. When your young teen has damaged someone's personal property, he should be responsible for fixing or replacing that property. Doesn't that make sense?

Fighting with Friends/Siblings. Some fights are *Trivial Fights*:

- ☐ "You're on my side!"
- ☐ "She's breathing my air!"
- ☐ "He hit me!"

Teens turn these arguments on and off. At times they argue because they're hungry, tired, bored or confused. It's almost impossible to discover who started it or why it began. Just stay cool; the kids really love each other.

A few fights are *Topic Fights*:

- ☐ "Butter is not good for you!"
- ☐ "My friend said so!" "Well, then she's wrong!"

☐ "Jackson bats 250." "No, he doesn't. He bats 350!"

It doesn't take long for the kids to realize that they will have differences of opinion — that's OK. These kind of arguments become verbal debates.

Some fights are *Attack Fights*:

☐ "Give that back, you turkey!"

☐ "I said, get out of my room!"

☐ "You jerk, stay out of my life!"

These fights can lead to hitting, kicking and biting. For sure, these fights result in name-calling and put-downs. Attack fights are harmful to the kids and destructive to the family atmosphere, so this kind of fight should be eliminated.

Parents can help by:

- Understanding why. The whys are like symptoms of something not being quite right. Parents could demand the fighting stop, but the cause may continue inside and undetected.
- Developing a positive home atmosphere. A positive home encourages positive feelings in all the family members. If the teens feel good about themselves, they will be more likely to feel good about others.
- Helping the kids learn to express anger constructively.

Jason and Cliff were yelling about Jason's records. They began calling each other names and throwing things in the room. Parents tend to use one of the following tactics in coping with this situation:

- Leave them alone. Let them fight it out. Of course this doesn't teach them much about getting along.
- "You guys have three minutes to solve your problem, or no phone privileges tonight." They will probably comply, but the real frustration is still there.
- Assuming the oldest to be responsible, Dad says, "Jason, I'm ashamed of you. You're the oldest; can't you act a little older?" Here the oldest learns that he gets blamed for everything. The youngest learns he can get away with anything.
- "OK! Calm down. Jason, you look pretty upset. Let's work this out. What are you angry about? Tell me how you feel. Cliff, tell me your side. How do you feel? Jason would you feel better about this if..." This models a constructive way to handle anger.

"I'm Not A Kid Anymore!"

Deciding About Tobacco. In several states the rage among boys 11-15 years old is trying smokeless tobacco. It seems that about half the young teens are trying dip, the stuff you put between your lower lip and gums. Somehow they think this stuff is safer. It's not.

Tobacco is still a messy problem. It has been proven to cause cancer, yet we continue to feed the habit. If your teen is using tobacco in any form, sit down and calmly discuss the problems you have with it. Discuss an appropriate plan for stopping the habit. It may take some pretty strong consequences to get the tobacco use stopped, but it must be done. The restriction of stereo and TV privileges is usually effective.

Deciding About Sex.   When there is pressure to be sexually active before marriage, a teenager has five choices. Which one would your teen choose?

☐ Give in.

☐ Say "no" because you are scared.

☐ Run.

☐ Say "no" because this is not the time.

☐ Thank God for the gift of sex, but keep it under wraps.

I know of at least eight reasons why your young teen should not be sexually active. You will undoubtedly think of others. Use this as a resource for writing a letter to your teen or for having a talk with your teen (or both).

- Being sexually active before marriage makes sex less special and sets you up to lose some of the potential ecstasy of sex.
- If you get involved sexually with the person you are dating, sex takes over the relationship.
- If you decide to be sexually active you will have to do something with the guilt. If it's not handled, it will cause sexual problems later on. Guilt by itself is powerful enough to leave us impotent.
- Sex for pleasure builds loneliness.
- Sex before marriage distracts from the key word used to describe marriage in the Bible—fidelity!
- Sex before marriage actually breaks up more relationships than it strengthens.
- Sex drives in the teen years need to be controlled because your emotions mature more

slowly than your body. Just because the sex
drive works doesn't mean you are ready to
use it.

- It is very easy to mix up your desires. You
  may really want affection and think that sex
  is the only way to get it. If you get healthy
  amounts of affection, you may find less
  problems controlling your sexual desires.

Deciding About Faith. Parents can shape their
teen's faith by doing these seven things:

1. Take your teen to church. The Sunday services,
   Bible classes, youth devotionals, special events,
   camps and other church times play a vital role in
   helping to shape faith.
2. Your teen needs to be around "faith" people—people
   who trust God for their future. Teens need to hear
   these people tell about what God is doing in their
   lives.
3. To shape the faith of teens you have to start where
   they are. Accept them right there, pimples and all,
   doubts and all.
4. Use the everyday moments to talk about God and
   his directing of your life. Problems, crises, routines
   and celebrations all fit together as a tapestry of
   learning events. Take advantage of the moments.
5. Help your teen get to know God. Encourage your
   teen to have a personal study time. Talk about God
   in personal terms and study the Bible as if you were
   learning more and more about a best friend. Spend
   special times praying with your youngster.
6. Look for the supernatural. Faith is seeing something that isn't there yet. If we are looking, God is

pointing out to us supernatural things we have never seen before.

7. Perhaps the most meaningful thing you can do is to tell your story. Make sure your teen knows how you came to the Lord, what kind of struggles you've had and what kind of victories you've received.

"You Don't Understand!"

Going Together. Most young teens don't talk to their parents about romantic things. They are very serious when they say, "You don't understand." In fact, teens doubt that anyone feels what they feel. It would not be unheard of for a young teen to say, "You don't know what love is; you have never loved like I love!" Have patience and accept their biased view with grace.

Breaking Up. A break-up is like an emotional amputation. You can help your teen cope with the loss by:

- Accepting it as painful, real and over.
- Helping him talk about the pain. Pain is a sign of healing. It is absolutely essential to feel it and talk about it.
- Getting your teen back with his friends. Encourage him to go with a same sex friend to work out, run or participate in some other physical activity.
- Telling him he'll know that the relationship is finished when he can walk past that person in the hall and say "Hi" without it bringing up all the hurt feelings. Reassure him that it will be possible.
- Getting your teen busy doing something for someone else. Giving him responsibilities will take his mind off the rejection.

Silence.   There are times when teens want their parents out of their hair. Under normal circumstances, let their silence be. Don't expect your young teen to talk with you about all the things he talked about as a child. It is important to note, however, that silence is one of the first warning signs of depression. Read more on this in Chapter 10.

Distrust.   Three turtles decided to go to the beach for a picnic. One was to bring the food, the other the drinks and the third turtle was to carry the umbrella. They got about halfway there when the turtle who was supposed to have the drinks discovered that he had forgotten the ice chest. One of his buddies suggested that the forgetful turtle should go back and get the drinks, and the other two would wait there.

"No, you'll go on without me!"

"No, we won't. You go on! We'll wait right here."

So the forgetful turtle left, and the two buddies rested by a big rock. They waited two days...three days... and on the fourth day one of them turned to the other and suggested, "Well, I think we'd better go on. I don't think he's coming back."

Just then out from behind a rock came the forgetful turtle crying out, "I knew you wouldn't wait. I knew it! I knew it!"

During these early teen years your teen is a lot like a turtle. At times he will stick his neck out and make a lot of progress; at other times he will pull inside his shell and hide away. Either way his peers have conditioned him to be distrustful of adults in general and parents specifically. So if you have the distrustful turtle living with you, shoot straight with him. Don't give him simple answers to complex questions. Talk it out; honesty is the only way to counteract distrust.

ALMOST GROWN

Living with young teenagers is a challenging experience. Every part of life is lived with intensity. When they are down, they're really down, and when they're up, they're flying. Don't push them into adulthood before their time.

Listen to them speak. There is a hidden message behind every word. Give them the chance to make their own decisions about important things. Expect some failure and some pain. Let them learn from their mess-ups; don't spend your time rescuing them. And, look for ways to open discussion and build trust.

9

Put the Monkey on Their Backs

15-18 Years

High schoolers remind me of satellites. They are *very* expensive to launch. Each day is spent circling just out of reach of the launch area. Invariably, the communications link fouls up, or there is a malfunction and the circuits go haywire. If communication actually stops, it must be due to some sort of electrical interference.

Satellites are connected with ground control and yet are independent of the Earth's environment. It has taken years of development to prepare them for their destiny—to fly freely, but with a purpose. The Ausubels, prominant researchers in the adolescent years, have suggested an interesting theory of adolescent development along the satellite concept.

After years of testing, teenagers should be ready for the freedom to fly, make mistakes and find their purpose while still living within the limitations of their home. To do this they need to have the monkey of responsibility on their back. They need to feel the load and the joy of living with the monkey.

Keeping the monkey on the teenager's back helps him to develop independence, learn to cope with his anxieties and discover how to manage conflict. Remember, it is the goal of Common Sense Discipline to help parents raise children who have learned how to take charge of their own lives. You will find structure and limitations are still needed, although the most reliable structure now will be your teen's own conscience. Setting the limits is still your job. Rules and limits are like old friends, comforting to have around, and always there if you need them. And, you will still need them.

WHO'S IN CHARGE

In order for a teenager to be in charge of his own life, he must know what to do with at least three monkeys.

1. The monkey of independence — This means responsibility must shift from the parent to the teen. The monkey must come off our backs and jump onto his back.
2. The monkey of anxiety — This means the teen must know what to do with his worries and emotional concerns. No one can do another person's worrying for him, but through the years parents have sure tried.
3. The monkey of conflict — This means the teen must know how to appropriate ways to work out differences and make adjustments. Some adults still don't know what to do with this monkey.

Chart 6 recommends that most of the decisions during these later years be made by the teen. Putting the monkey on his back will force him to take responsibility for his successes and face the consequences of his failures. You will still find it necessary to place limits on activities and determine appropriate consequences. Don't forget to look

Common Sense Discipline Chart 6

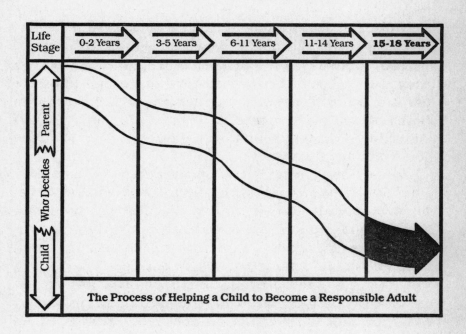

Life Stage	0-2 Years	3-5 Years	6-11 Years	11-14 Years	15-18 Years

The Process of Helping a Child to Become a Responsible Adult

for things he is doing right. Expecting the best in your teen will help him develop an "I can" attitude toward conquering any tough problem.

DEVELOPING INDEPENDENCE

Setting Goals

You can help your teenager become more independent by encouraging him to set his own goals and then giving him the freedom to work toward those goals.

Leo Randolph had what many people would call an unrealistic goal. For years he had trained to be the best.

Leo wanted to win a gold medal in the 1976 Olympics. The experts didn't give Leo a chance. He was only eighteen years old, and he had no experience on the international level.

But Leo had an undeniable drive to achieve the gold. He had a poster-size picture taken of himself with a gold medal around his neck. That poster was positioned so that every morning when Leo opened his eyes the first thing he saw was Leo with the gold and a caption, "Leo Randolph Wins Gold Medal." It worked.

Leo won the 112-pound boxing class! He had motivation, training and a goal.

What does your teen have on the poster in his mind? What does he want to do with his life? What choices is he thinking about? By the way, in an interview with his hometown newspaper, Leo said that winning the gold was a great moment in his life, but the greatest moment was when he became a Christian several years earlier.

Arrange a date with your teen. Spend the first part of the date catching up with what's happening in his world. When the time is right (God will help you know when, if you ask), tell about a goal you had when you were in high school, and ask your teen to share some of his goals. Be sure that you just listen. Even if you disagree with one of the goals, now is the time to listen. You can debate the morality or practicality later.

Priority on Privacy

When it comes to privacy, some parents are uncomfortable putting the monkey on the teenager's back. During adolescence teens are very sensitive about their privacy needs; also parents are very suspicious about what goes on in private. I believe some teens deliberately leave their rooms a mess because they think that will keep Mom out.

They will pay the price of the hassle if they can keep Mom out, thus having their privacy.

The Bedroom

One of my best friends has a teenage daughter, who has a typical problem with her room. Let me describe it. Posters overlap to completely cover one wall of Abby's room. Fingernail polish, old movie tickets, ribbons from the pep rally, notes from friends, records, discarded makeup and a bag of corn chips are stacked and scattered over the desk top. Hanging on the closet door are three sets of clothes she tried on this morning before deciding what to wear. The stereo is having its own jam session playing the same album over and over. Pillows and stuffed animals are stacked on top of the bed. Her mirror is edged with notes from Danny. Danny's autographed picture is stuck at lip level on the mirror. Somewhere among the animals, clothes and record albums is a telephone — her daily life-line to the teen world.

This is the place where Abby talks, studies, plans, thinks, dreams, prays and cries. It's her private world. She considers her room to be as private as her mail, her phone calls and her diary. And she feels she ought to be free to keep her room just the way she wants.

Just as we arrived there recently, I overheard... "Abby Elaine Thomason, you get in here right now and get this room of yours straightened, before company comes, or you can consider yourself grounded for the whole weekend!"

Embarrassed, Abby ran back down the hall. Her privacy had been challenged, so she defended herself, "My room is just like I like it!"

"I've told you before what I think of your backtalk, young lady. You're grounded for this weekend, and if you say another word you're grounded for a month!" Mom was a bit out of control.

Abby slammed her door, turned up the stereo, and, I'm sure, talked to herself about how unfair her mother was. "I can't wait to get out of this house where I can be on my own!"

At the beginning of this conflict a slight change of words might have avoided the ensuing battle.

"Abby, we've got company, and I'm in a real time squeeze. I know they won't be in your room, but would you at least pick up the big chunks? It doesn't have to pass inspection, but I would sure feel more at ease."

This way the issue stays centered on the room cleaning and "how clean is clean" and not on a developing power struggle between Mom and Abby. In order for Mom to feel comfortable making these changes, she must be able to accept the fact that Abby might like her private world a little more cluttered than Mom does.

Abby must realize that her room is connected to the other rooms in the house and should meet the same general standards as the rest of the house. If she does not respond by keeping up to those standards then some appropriate consequences are in order. Limited use of "family" property like the car or phone might be of help.

Accepting Personal Likes

Another monkey with which parents have difficulty is coping with personal likes and dislikes of their teenagers. There are three hallmarks of independence that parents in every generation have trouble accepting:

Fashion — You may have noticed that in the push for separation from their parents' culture, teenagers won't be caught dead wearing something that's not accepted by their culture. The "geeks" would stay home before they would dress in the fashion of the "preps."

Music — I have divided teens into groups by asking what radio stations they listen to most often. There is security in knowing everyone likes your favorite music. In many ways the Top Ten songs help some teens decide what they are supposed to like. So, generally with music, independence is measured by how different it is from old fogies' music.

Friends — Sometimes our own flesh and blood will pick the most unusual characters as friends. You may find you don't know why you dislike this latest friend, or you may know exactly:

- ☐ clothes
- ☐ breath
- ☐ hair
- ☐ language
- ☐ laughter
- ☐ none of the above
- ☐ all of the above

You may have a socially conscious teen who is seriously trying to touch human need. Or your teen may be eagerly trying to be evangelistic with God's message of grace.

Even though you want to honor the independence of your teen, you have not abdicated your place as parent. You still have an obligation to intervene when you suspect personal welfare is at stake. In fact there will be times when you *have* to intervene. Intervening means you impose pre-set family rules concerning behavior or speech. For example:

☐ "No one in this family buys or plays music that has dirty or erotic lyrics. Those records must go!"

☐ "All members of this family are free to choose their own clothes as long as they are decent and will not embarrass the rest of us!"

☐ "In this family we select our best friends from people who share our beliefs about God and the Christian lifestyle."

When a teen's personal preferences violate the values of your family, try this discussion:

☐ "You know I love you and I always will. I want you to know how proud I am of you and the way you are growing up. But I am concerned about your friend, Richard. Can we talk about him? He looks like a doper to me; is he?"

☐ "If he is a doper let's find some way to help him, if he wants help. Ask him over and let's both talk with him. If he refuses help, then I believe you need to break off the friendship. What do you think?"

Sometimes you discover personal preferences long after they've become a habit. Dealing with a record collection of lewd and erotic music, one parent tried this:

"Craig, I just happened to listen to the words of that album you had on last night. Are you aware of the words? They are just not acceptable in this house. Let's talk about what we can do about this."

"I don't want to censor everything you listen to, and I won't, but I believe that album should be destroyed. I'll tell you what. If you'll destroy the album, I will give you enough money to replace it with one with acceptable lyrics. Deal?"

Parents make an enormous mistake by writing off contemporary music. There are a surprising number of wholesome songs. Condemning all of it will likely cause your children to embrace it all the more.

When your teen is tied into a complicated, unhealthy web of relationships and absolutely nothing seems to work, consider moving. Though there are enormous financial burdens, it has worked well for many who made this decision due to harmful relationships. The teen then has a chance to establish a new identity, free of negative influences.

Asking questions and listening, regardless of the answers, will help you do the best thing for your teen. So many parents don't listen. Parents who don't listen build a wall of resentment in their teen's heart.

Questions help the teen to search his own mind and to think about the answers (even if he gives you a glib response at the time). Listening beyond the words builds respect.

Sometimes compromises are necessary, and at times parents should accept differences in personal preference without comment. This strategy may destroy the motivation for the questionable behavior in the first place (getting the parent shook may have been the goal).

Freedom and the Automobile

For the typical high school kid in America, getting a driver's license is a rite of passage to independence—"At last I am free!" I asked a perceptive sixteen-year-old boy, "What's so great about having your own car?"

He replied, "Having a car is better than having a room of your own. In a car you are free, you can get away from the house. I feel grown up just riding around with a friend — as long as there is no adult in the car. While you're driving you can play the stereo as loud as you want and nobody yells at you.

"Having a car makes me feel like a man. Sometimes I like to show off a little. Don't tell my dad that I should pay for the tires. Cuttin' up a little shows everybody that I'm in control. Nobody is telling me what to do. I am making the decisions; I have the power. I think that's why girls are always interested in your car.

"There's something thrilling about the risk of driving fast on a mountain road or seeing how fast my machine will go. My car is more than just a set of wheels. It's kinda like a part of my body."

Listen carefully to the words of this boy. He is telling you something that might jog your memory of days long gone by. Your high schooler will probably never tell you these things. Accept them as truth; it will help you understand what's happening as your teen begins a love affair with his car.

Trust Your Teenager as a Driver

- Spend time riding in the car while your teen is driving. The more you know of his skills the more you will trust him.

- Conduct regular maintenance checks on the cars your family owns. Everyone should know the basics about the car — like the difference between the radiator and the carburetor.

- Develop a list of safety rules for your whole family.
- Talk openly about driving experiences. Share your mess-ups and encourage your teen to share his.
- If your teen has a car of his own, he should be responsible for its upkeep, its operation and its cost.
- Realize it takes time to trust, so be patient.

An automobile is a challenge to any teenager's self-control. If he knows you are aware of how much the car means to him and you are flexible where you can be, your teen will be, too. He will be as self-controlled in the car as you are.

Drinking and Driving. According to the National Highway Safety Administration, arrests of teens for drunk driving have tripled since 1960, and accidents are the leading cause of death for 15-24 year olds in America. Of course, you know we have a problem with teenage drinking and driving because you pay the insurance premiums.

I believe driving demands alertness and self-control, so I have these words for my son Lane...

"Lane, I don't want you riding in a car if I don't know the driver. If I've never met the driver, please introduce us. You know me well enough to know that if the driver ever appears stoned or drunk or goofy (more than the usual teenager), you'll have to get another ride or stay home. While we're on the subject, anytime a driver of a car you're in starts to drink, ask if you can get out as soon as possible. Call me, and I'll come get you.

Lane, if you ever drink while you're the driver, do not under any circumstance drive. Call me, and I'll come and get you! No hassles till the next day."

Making Decisions On Their Own

The best way to help your teenager make decisions for himself is to keep the monkey on his back. Give him situations where he has to decide, where he has the opportunity to fail. The Bible puts it this way: "It is good for a man to bear the yoke while he is young. Let him sit alone in silence, for the Lord has laid it on him. Let him bury his face in the dust — there may yet be hope" (Lamentations 3:27-29).

I know some teenagers who don't make any decisions concerning their lives. They just go along with whomever they're with. If it feels OK, do it. By high school teens should be making most of their decisions for themselves. Here's how to help your kid do just that.

Checklist For Helping Teens Make Decisions

Every decision can be evaluated on the basis of two dimensions:

1. Quality — Is it important that the decision be right, true to values and beliefs — the best choice?
2. Acceptance—Is it important that the decision be accepted by others?

For example, after a youth gathering the gang decides to go for pizza. You've been told to come straight home and not go anywhere else. Do you:

a. Go with the gang and tell your Mom it was a long meeting?

> b. Leave and go straight home because you're not hungry?
> c. Call Dad and ask to stay out for the pizza time?
> d. Convince the gang to have the pizza delivered so you can stay and eat?

Solution "a" is a decision based on acceptance, not quality.

Solution "b" shows neither acceptance nor quality was important in the decision.

Solution "c" is a decision based on quality.

Solution "d" shows that both quality and acceptance were important in the decision.

It's essential to determine if this situation calls for a quality or acceptance decision or both. If neither is important then a conscientious decision is not required.

Now that you have evaluated your situation and you're considering what's important — quality or acceptance — it's time to ask God for wisdom. Ask and believe that God will give you wisdom. Then get ready for it (James 1:5).

- ✔ Become a listener. Pay attention to the feeling hidden between the lines (James 1:19).

- ✔ Help your teen think of alternatives. Write them all down.

- ✔ Ask the "What would happen" question. What would happen if you decided to...(option a)...(option b), etc.? Get your teen to evaluate and describe the possibilities.

- ✔ Don't make the decision for your teen. If he asks you what you would do, tell him what you'd do and why—only if asked!

- ✔ If you make a wrong decision, it's not the end of the world. Everyone falls on his face in the dust. That's the way it always has been, and that's the way it always will be.

COPING WITH ANXIETY

Not long ago the National Institute of Mental Health announced that the number one mental health problem for adults in America is anxiety. You don't have to have the NIMH do a study to discover that among high school-aged teenagers anxiety is considered to be a top priority mental health problem. We're in great shape, parents and teens both worrying all the time. It's too bad there isn't a way to worry away our weight. We would all be skinny.

Parents worry if the kids are dating, and then they worry if they're not. Parents worry when the grades are bad, and then they worry if the grades are all good. Parents even worry when the kid gets a job, and they'll worry when he doesn't have a job. No wonder anxiety is rated number one.

Understanding The Silent Worries

We don't talk much about our worries. Our struggle with anxiety is usually a covert struggle, one that goes on behind the doors of our mind. Most of our fears are imaginary fears — what if...concerns. We don't want others to know we have that kind of fear. So we spend our free hours in front of a TV set or plugged into a stereo, not because we are interested in the pictures or the words. We do it to escape, to hide from our anxieties.

Teens especially seem to be fighting for the worry monkey, and once they get the monkey, they either pretend he's not there or spend all their time playing with him.

Consider the following teenagers:

A sixteen-year-old girl, typically shy and plain-looking, worries that she will never get married and that she will be a virgin forever. She dreams daily about meeting the "perfect" young man who loves her for the beauty she has buried beneath her shyness.

An eighteen-year-old senior is anxious about his grades. He needs to have a 3.5 overall grade average to get the scholarship he needs for college. His whole future is in the hands of Mr. Brumbley, his government teacher. He needs an "A," and Brumbley only gives a couple of A's a year.

A 17-year-old high-strung, easily-irritated cheerleader is worried about her boyfriend. He is too possessive and demanding. She is ready to break up with him, but he is the most popular guy at Central High. Nobody has ever broken up with him before. What will her friends think?

I think it is important for teens and parents to understand the anxieties teenagers face. The three examples above are real, and the anxieties are real. Teens tell me they worry about:

- ☐ grades
- ☐ friends
- ☐ romantic relationships
- ☐ jobs
- ☐ future
- ☐ parents

We should encourage teenagers to get in touch with their worries, and then get rid of the monkey. You don't have to have the worry monkey on your back. Give the little critter to God. Put the monkey on his back. The Bible promises, "Humble yourselves, therefore, under God's mighty hand, that he may lift you up in due time. Cast all your anxiety on him because he cares for you" (I Peter 5:6,7).

Talk On Worry

After a time of prayer with God, set aside some one-on-one time with your youngster and tell him about a worry that is bugging you. Follow this guideline:

- ☐ Accept the fear or worry as yours—"Yes, I am worried."

- ☐ Pray with your teen, giving your worry to God.

- ☐ Talk to your kid about the worry. Describe it.

- ☐ Discuss ways that God can help you give up the monkey.

- ☐ Ask your teen to pray for you.

- ☐ Expect to be relieved of the worry. Look for peace.

HANDLING CONFLICT

Conflict is fascinating. Your task, should you choose to accept it, is to infiltrate your teenager's heart and convince him there are better ways to handle conflict than winning, losing or refusing to play the game.

Of course, this can be a frustrating task. Your son or daughter may be really happy with the way he/she handles conflict. Then what do you do?

You may find that after your best effort, your teen still has not heard what you have been trying to say. Remember, the fence is still up. You are still the parent; you are still responsible for your teen's growth. Firm consequences can help the teen break through to reality and get his act together. Here again, consequences related to the use of the car, the phone, or other family property seem to work best. Working through even the tough times can end up bringing us closer together.

Discuss Controversial Issues

Your teen probably knows what you are against, but does he know why? You can be assured that by the time he finishes high school your teen will know someone who has had to deal personally with the problems of drugs, homosexuality and abortion. It's not enough for parents to use scare tactics about taboo subjects. In fact, that's exactly the wrong thing to do. Instead, when a controversial issue comes up, be willing to sit down and discuss both sides of it.

Teens make smarter decisions when they have factual information and have talked through the issue. Ask your teen to make a list of controversial issues. You make one, too. Then plan a family issues night. You might want to invite others in for your discussion evening. Remember, you are not trying to defend what you believe; you are simply rapping on topics of concern.

The topics of concern could deal with:

- ☐ Ethics
- ☐ Religion
- ☐ Politics
- ☐ Evolution
- ☐ War
- ☐ Capital Punishment
- ☐ Drugs

☐ Sex

☐ Death

☐ Abortion

☐ Pornography

This kind of discussion night will be a great opportunity to practice your listening skills. Please don't turn the time into an evening of anger and argument. The goal is to listen.

Curfew Conflict

One afternoon in chemistry class several teens were comparing notes on how strict and unfair parents are about curfews. In the middle of this negative discussion Barbara stated, "You don't know how lucky you are. I just wish my mother cared enough to set a curfew for me. The best I get is, 'See ya when you get home.' Then when I get home, she's always asleep. I think it would be kinda nice to have someone waiting up for me when I get in, someone to hassle me a little, and someone who cared where I was and when I was coming home."

Poor Barbara had a better understanding of her need for limits than her mother did. Setting a curfew is a covert way of saying, "We love you."

Telling a teen, "See ya when you get home," is like telling a four-year-old, "Stop eating cookies when you've had enough." Although teens need to have input, it is unrealistic to expect them to set their own curfew limits.

Here are some guidelines to help you set curfews. These times have been suggested by Ann Landers:

☐ 10th grade - 10:00 pm

☐ 11th grade - 11:00 pm

☐ 12th grade - 12:00 am

If your teen has trouble getting in before the pre-set curfew, then determine a consequence that is time related. For example, because he came in one hour late he will have to come in one hour earlier next time.

Critical Attitude

I wonder what would happen if we spent as much time affirming our teens as we do criticizing them? You can be sure of one thing. No matter how bad you think your teens are, there are plenty of parents who would love to trade problems with you, if not the kids themselves. Expect your teens to be and do their best, and they'll want to live up to your expectations.

Recently a mother complained that she and her daughter had a heated discussion over what clothes the daughter could wear to church on Wednesday night. "What can I do about it?" she asked.

"I would celebrate. Are you sure that's all you're upset about?" I replied.

"No, she is a great kid. I just think she should dress nicer."

"Listen, I hate to break it to you, but where do you think most of the kids in her high school are on Wednesday nights? Are they in church? And of those who are in church, how many of them want to be there? I want to encourage you to go home and tell your daughter how pleased you are with her desire to attend church, regardless of what she wears."

If your teen is critical all the time, try shocking the conversation with some affirming statements. Keep it up for a week or two, and I guarantee different results. Try:

- "I know you put lots of effort into your grades, and I really respect you for working so hard."
- "Ever since the day I brought you home from the hospital I've been thankful that you're my daughter."
- "You really have a pleasing way about you. I admire the kindness you show others."
- "Thanks for being such a cooperative kid. I know some of the hassles you are facing right now, and I think you have really developed great self-control."
- "Thanks for being so forgiving of me when I mess up."

Going to Church

Although perfect attendance at church is not a requirement for getting through the pearly gates, it can be a problem in some families. Parents have the responsibility to require their teens to go to church as often as the family goes. It is not an option as long as the teens still live at home. I believe in that responsibility.

At the same time I believe that flexibility is needed in each situation. Find out what's buggin' them about church and fix what can be fixed, realizing up front that faith cannot be forced. If you have questions, reread the "I'm Not a Kid Anymore" section on junior high (chapter 8).

WHERE IS THE MONKEY?

The ultimate goal of Common Sense Discipline is to help parents and teachers raise resourceful children who will become responsible adults. When this goal is accomplished, the monkey has been successfully placed on the teenager's back for good, and we call him adult.

In order for the goal to be reached, years of patience and faith must be punctuated by letting children make decisions, permitting them to fail, listening to their struggle, helping them succeed and setting limits where appropriate. At times it is frightening, but it can be one of the greatest adventures of your life. Remember, even after the teens are gone, you can still catch them doing something right!

10

Tackling the Tough Times

11-18 Years

CRISIS CAN BRING YOU TOGETHER

Instead of pulling you apart, crisis can push you together. When you face a crisis with your kids, look for the pathway that can bring you together. It's always there, although many times well-hidden. I pray that you will have eyes to see it. As we examine problem times, keep your eyes open.

Teenage Depression

Warning signs:

- [ ] Change in eating habits
- [ ] Feeling helpless
- [ ] Losing interest in doing things
- [ ] Sleeplessness
- [ ] Sudden outbursts of crying
- [ ] Serious drop in grades

203

☐ Extreme fatigue

☐ Increased isolation from friends or family

☐ Feeling of "nobody understands"

☐ Expressing hostility

Although everyone occasionally feels down or sad, some of us, especially teens, go through periods of depression. If you sense that your teenager is suffering from more than just temporary sadness, try getting him or her to:

☐ Take in a movie

☐ Fix something that's broken

☐ Care for someone's pet

☐ Exercise

☐ Learn a new game

It may be that these suggestions don't help. In that case, see a professional counselor immediately. The chances are your teen is thinking about or has considered suicide.

Attempted Suicide

Teens who attempt to kill themselves do it thinking that suicide is a way to solve their problems:

☐ No one understands.

☐ No one appreciates me.

☐ I'm just a puppet; my parents hold the strings.

☐ I feel pressure to be tough.

☐ Life is frustrating and unfair.

☐ I'm lonely.

Communication is the first step toward prevention. Crisis hotlines can provide this first step. Ask your telephone operator for the crisis help or suicide hotline in your area.

If your teenager tells you he or she has a plan of suicide, call a counselor or the hotline immediately. Don't take a threat casually.

Legal Problems

If your teen gets into legal trouble, *never*, never allow him to spend the night in jail on a first arrest. Consult your attorney as soon as possible and go down and post bond quietly. Avoid a scene in front of the police; save the lectures for later.

If your teen is letting traffic tickets pile up but does nothing about paying them, demand that he pay the tickets or forfeit the use of any car. Tell him you expect him to abide by the law as long as he lives under your roof because everyone under your roof abides by the law.

Occasionally, parents whose teen has been arrested three or four times will ask my advice. After discovering that the parents have paid his bail each time and the teen's behavior has not changed, it's time to face the consequences. Since he's a legal adult and certainly knows what the score is, if he gets into trouble with the police again, he probably needs to face the music. That means no material help from his parents.

That means letting him arrange for his own bail and attorney or take his chances with a court-appointed attorney if he can't afford another one. After all, since he's been arrested three times already, he certainly knows what to expect, but he's never had to experience the consequences because someone always bailed him out of trouble.

It is important up front for parents to express their love but to be firm. Bailing him out of trouble only prevents him from learning from the consequences of his actions. Should he be arrested again, assure him that you'll visit him in jail but that he'll have to arrange how to get out without your help.

Drinking

It's my understanding that the number one drug problem in America today is alcohol abuse. Marijuana and cocaine get lots of attention, but booze is still number one.

If your teen comes home high or drunk, lay out some hard logical consequences for drinking. (Don't try to talk while he is drunk.) For example, you might ground your teen for a weekend; tell him if he comes home high again, he will be grounded for four weekends. Tell him you expect him to remain sober so long as he lives under your roof. As a safety measure, promise him that if he gets high in the future or is with a friend who's driving who can't drive safely, to call you and you'll come get him without making a hassle. The important thing is that your teen still feels like he can call you when he needs help.

Drugs

If you suspect your teen is involved with drugs, get professional help immediately. Ask your physician about local drug abuse programs where parents can get advice and information. If your physician knows of no such programs, contact hospitals, mental health centers and social service agencies by looking in the phone book. Help is available, so keep asking. Attend meetings and participate in these programs. Get more information about what you can and can't do to help your child. Ask questions, get sound advice and then follow it.

Often, the people who can best help drug abusers are recovered abusers themselves, much the same way members of Alcoholics Anonymous help each other.

Never, *never* kick a child out of the house when you suspect a drug abuse or an emotional problem. When kids get into the habit of abusing privileges or taking advantage of their parents' good will, some action needs to be taken, but not all at once and not without serious consideration to possible consequences. The problems that run beneath drug abuse go much deeper than the surface, and counseling by experienced professionals is always needed.

I worked once with a couple whose son was on drugs and refused to cooperate in any way with them. Eventually he moved out of their house and in with a girlfriend who had her own apartment. His parents were beside themselves about what to do. In the meantime, he became dependent on drugs and began to skip school.

Finally his lifestyle caught up with him, and he was arrested for DWI and drug possession. Due to his age he was released back into the custody of his parents. In a subsequent court hearing he was placed on probation and ordered to live at home, attend school and stay away from his girlfriend, who apparently was his drug supplier.

As soon as the court hearing was over, he immediately moved back in with his girlfriend and things quickly went downhill. What should his parents do?

I told his parents he certainly seemed to be playing some sort of "I dare you to stop me" game, since the first thing he did after being placed on probation was violate it by moving back in with his girlfriend. To ignore his age and his drug abuse would only allow his problems to get worse. "Why don't you just turn it over to the authorities who are better prepared for dealing with problems like this than you are?"

WHEN A TEENAGER SAYS "NO!"

Occasionally a teenager will become totally uncooperative and disobedient. It's as though he is testing you to see if you're still willing to lead. If you're not, he'll take over. In one case, where drugs were not an issue, parents of a rebellious son consulted a therapist. This was their decision: One day while their son was at school, both parents went to his room and stripped it completely. He was left with his bed, dresser and the clothes in his closet. Gone were his posters, stereo and records and other assorted junk. When he came home that afternoon, he stared at his room in disgust and then turned angrily to his parents and demanded, "Where's my stuff?"

They replied something like this: "We put your things in storage boxes in the attic for safe keeping. If you want your things back, you will have to earn them back, one at a time, by acting more courteous with us and cooperating around the house. If you don't want to cooperate with us, your things will remain in storage."

In just a few short days the teen became more responsible and polite. Gradually he earned back his things by negotiating with his parents, finding out what was expected of him, and then acting better around the house. Now, a number of years later, he's grown and a fine young man. Most parents would consider him a source of pride, now. But for a while the situation looked desperate. Parents need to remember: *Desperate situations call for desperate action.*

SEX FOR THE WRONG REASONS

Teenagers get involved sexually for a lot of reasons. Many times the bottom line is not love. The following list of reasons has been compiled from interviews with teens who are active sexually.

1. Affection—Seeking sexual intimacy out of a desire for closeness.
2. Animosity—Venting hostility toward parents by having sex with someone.
3. Anxiety—Using sex as a temporary relief from frustrations.
4. Boredom—Seeking sex as a momentary break from a boring routine.
5. Mending wounds—Using sex as a way to make up after an argument or to forget one's troubles.
6. Accomplishments—Keeping up with peers or "scoring," because it seems to be what is expected.
7. Recreation—Engaging in sex for the fun of it.
8. Lust—Engaging in sex to relieve sexual hunger.

If Your Daughter Is Pregnant

If your daughter tells you she thinks she's pregnant, before you even try to decide on a plan of action, first have her examined by a physician. Girls have been known to miss periods, and maybe yours will be lucky. If she is pregnant, here are some options for you and your daughter to consider:

1. Remain single and allow the baby to be adopted.
2. Remain single and allow the baby to be raised by other relatives.
3. Remain single and keep the baby.
4. Marry and keep the baby.

Adoption

Placing the baby for adoption can be accomplished by your daughter finishing her pregnancy at home and attending her own school or completing the school year with home-bound teachers until delivery. Or you can arrange for your daughter to live away from home until after the birth by: 1) staying in a home for unwed mothers, 2) staying in an approved foster home, or 3) staying in informal foster care with a relative or trusted friend.

To learn more about any of these options, talk with a social worker. You can ask your physician, minister or a Social Service Agency listed in the Yellow Pages for more information. Usually there is no charge for this consultation, and it will ease your worries to talk things over with someone who has helped others with this problem.

Keeping the Baby

Some parents want to help their daughter raise her baby at home or place it with other relatives out of a sense of obligation. Usually I discourage this decision. To encourage a teenager to keep an unplanned, out-of-wedlock baby is like having one child raise another one. It's one thing for teenage girls to baby-sit, but raising a child on a full-time basis is something altogether different.

Marriage

The subsequent divorce rate for teenagers who married because they were pregnant is about 90%. Due to the problems, such as resentment and almost certain divorce, I wouldn't even give this option serious thought. My advice is this: Parents, if you really love that baby, arrange for adoption through a legitimate child care agency; then wait for grandkids that are planned and wanted.

DROPPING OUT OF SCHOOL

Sometimes teenagers do so poorly in school and fail so much that, in frustration, they decide to drop out. There are few things which cause teachers and parents more anguish. If your teenager is threatening to drop out of school, definitely seek professional counseling. Both of you could probably benefit from several sessions together. Even if he won't go, you go. It will be money well spent.

Dropping out of school or leaving home against your wishes recalls the words from Ecclesiastes: "There is a time for everything, and a season for every activity under heaven:...a time to embrace and a time to refrain,...a time to be silent and a time to speak..."(Ecc. 3). This may be one of those times to be silent after all the useful words have been said. It would be wonderful if all children graduated from high school and then had realistic plans for a job, college or military or vocational training. But, unfortunately, some of them leave school before it's time.

The prodigal son (Luke 15) was such a case. Apparently he had all the benefits of a good family, but one day he decided to leave it all. The scriptures give no record of anything his father might have said to stop him from going, though I can imagine what many parents would be tempted to say: "Don't you think this is premature? Are you sure you want to do this? Look, let's talk about it. I think you're getting ready to make the biggest mistake of your life." But no such arguments are recorded. Instead, the prodigal's father, recognizing there was little he could do or say to keep his son from leaving, decided to split the inheritance between his two sons. The youngest went on his way without hearing so much as, "You're going to be sorry."

After the boy had made the inevitable mess of his life, he returned home begging forgiveness and seeking only shelter and a job as a hired hand. Fortunately for him, his father's forgiveness was complete; his family relationship and his future were restored.

Like this father, parents have times when there aren't *good* decisions to make, only *painful* ones, from which they must pick the best of the bad choices at hand. Like the decision of a surgeon faced with amputation of an infected limb or doing nothing and allowing an infection to spread, sometimes parents have to pick the lesser of the two unpleasant choices. That's what the prodigal's father did.

Notice that the father didn't throw his son's failure up to him or say, "I told you so." Remaining silent is a painful decision to make, especially when we think our kids are about to make the mistake of their lives; sometimes being silent is the best thing to do. Occasionally rebellion has to take its course before repentance can come about.

LOOKING BACK

We've talked about lots of different problems in this chapter. Hopefully, your family will never need this information, but occasionally you do have those blown-out tires on a vacation. So I want you to be prepared if you have a problem. In my practice I've seen that no family is immune to problems. Parents who attend church regularly sometimes seem shocked when they discover a major problem in their family and are often reluctant to seek help until things can wait no longer. Often I hear the phrase, "I feel like if I were just a better Christian or prayed more then I wouldn't be having these problems." I try to reassure these parents that being a good Christian doesn't immunize one against broken bones or heart attacks; neither does it lessen the chance of emotional and behavioral problems. I wish it did, but it doesn't.

The problems do, however, give us a chance to see our weaknesses and discover God's strengths. The bad times *can* bring us closer together. Never stop praying for eyes to see the pathway of reconciliation. God can melt even the most stubborn heart. He is in the business of turning hearts of children to their parents and the hearts of parents to their young (Malachi 4:5,6).

11

Differences Build Confidence in Kids

The waitress had just poured our second cup of coffee when Gary explained, "As I see it there are four things that are certain: God is still in charge! Dead people don't bleed! I'll never make enough money! And no two kids are put together the same!"

Judy responded, "I'm glad our kids are different. It would be boring to be just like someone else. Every morning would begin with, 'Are you real or are you Memorex?'"

Judy has the right attitude about differences. It's our differences that make us special. Each youngster has distinctive differences in birth order, experiences, problems, energy, agenda, boundary requirements and abilities. The sooner you are able to recognize and accept your youngsters' differences, the sooner you will be able to help them use their differences as building blocks for confidence.

PERSONALITY AND BIRTH ORDER

Being first, second or third in the family line-up tends to affect a child's personality, regardless of what the parents do. If you're wondering which place is best, the truth is that there's good news and bad news for any position. As parents prepare themselves to raise thinking, responsible children, the first step is understanding that each child will be different. That's OK; in fact, it's good! The following descriptions of typical children are intended to point out the naturalness of differences. As you read, reflect on and evaluate your own situation.

Oldest Children

As a group, first-born children tend to walk, talk and do most of the "baby book" things earlier than other children. As the only child in the family, first-borns mostly have adults to copy, and so they strive to mimic grown-up actions early. Because there isn't an older brother or sister around to help them, oldies have to learn to do things for themselves.

First-time parents tend to be more cautious about the way they raise their first child. The oldest becomes a guinea pig in a new parenting system and so usually gets an overdose of protection. Consequently, first-born kids tend to be more cautious and conservative than their younger brothers and sisters. They tend to be higher achievers, more serious-minded, less sociable, generally make better grades and cause fewer problems in school. At times they seem to be model kids. Better watch out, though, because the pressure to be models — "But you're the oldest, and you know better! I can't believe *you* would do that!" — is hard for some kids to handle.

One disadvantage of being an oldest child is he generally has a "work" attitude about play and entertainment. First-borns tend to be compulsive about tasks and may have trouble relaxing or just doing nothing. They may accept the values and beliefs of parents without really questioning the concepts and making them their own.

First-Born Girls. Even in homes where both parents work outside the home, the first-born girl always gets an abundance of attention from Mom. While small, this daughter is around Mom almost without interruption and tries hard to be like Mom. Soon she becomes mother's little helper, and the pleasant remarks that Mom and Dad make about her helpful nature encourage her to act that way. It's no accident that most nurses and school teachers are oldest or only daughters. From their early years on, they copy the actions they see Mother do.

When brothers and sisters come along, some normal childhood jealousy is probably inevitable, but older girls soon discover that the surest way to lose favor with Mom and Dad is to be mean to the baby. At one time she had all of their attention, but now she has to share it with the baby. She discovers the way to get back into her parents' favor is to help out. Soon she learns to get diapers and brings them to Mom, tries to make the baby happy by bringing a toy and often tries to help with the bottle. Naturally, Mom appreciates all of this new source of help and continues to praise her little helper with remarks like, "You're a good big sister. You're Mother's best little helper." It's easy to see why so many nurses and teachers are oldest daughters.

First-Born Boys. The first-born son, whether he is the first or second child, tends to be more responsible and a higher achiever than later kids. After other children are born, he becomes the big brother and readily assumes that role, acting protective and sometimes bossy. Parents will frequently leave a small child in the care of an older brother at an age when they wouldn't think of allowing someone else in the neighborhood to baby-sit. Older boys tend to act more responsibly.

How many times have you heard well-meaning friends and relatives say to the older of two children, "You'd better watch out or your little brother will catch up with you." While this remark is usually said in jest when comparing height, the oldest is likely to take it literally and become worried about being passed by. To the youngest, a comment like that is music to his ears because nothing would suit him better than to be bigger. But the oldest doesn't want to lose his position, and so he works that much harder at excelling and achieving.

Even some of the family conflicts described in the Bible involve an older brother who felt outdone by a younger brother. Such was the case with Cain and Abel and with Esau and Jacob.

Middlers Are Moderates

Just as being the first child in a family leaves its imprint, so does being the second child. Second children generally are less academically oriented than oldest children but tend to be more socially adept. They grew up playing with two sets of friends—their own and their older brother's or sister's. Second children learn what works best with older and younger children and so get along well with all kinds of people. Because the oldest child had already carved out a niche in the family's history by being the first to walk, talk, go to school and ride a bike, the second child accepts that there are few firsts left for him. Consequently, he may go off on an entirely different tangent in his personality, if only to show his parents and others that "I'm different."

This difference is especially pronounced in elementary school where there have been several other children from the same family who did well. By the time junior comes along he's heard for the hundredth time, "Oh, so you're so and so's little brother/sister. I hope you're as smart as he/

she was." Better watch that line because it may be a set up for a "big" surprise. You see, that younger child has had to follow in big brother/sister's footsteps for so long that he's just dying to strike out on his own. When you tell him what you most admired about his older brother (grades, cooperation, attitudes, etc.), he's likely to do just the opposite to express his own individuality, if only to say, "I may have the same last name, but that's all we have in common." Remember, everyone is different.

The Baby Syndrome

Being the "baby" is tough. You gets lots of attention for being the youngest, and, of course, that feels good. But there is always an older brother or sister nearby who is impatient and wants you to hurry up. You can't help it if you're slow; you're just not grown-up yet. Older kids get impatient and rescue the youngest, saying, "Here, let me do it for you." After a time you decide to let them do your work because, "If you can't beat 'em, might as well join 'em." Since you have so many "parents" around telling you what to do, you sometimes tend to be more docile and passive. Youngest children tend to be more laid back and less achievement-oriented than their older brothers and sisters. At the same time, they also learn to manipulate those around them, like Jacob did Esau: "If they're going to treat me like a baby, at least I'm going to make it work for me on my terms." The baby of the family may find it most helpful to act helpless. It may be in the high school years before the youngest begins to assert himself.

Parents can foster this dependent attitude by developing a habit of rescuing their youngest. Children are frequently brought to my office with one problem or another, often school-related. I'll ask the child a question, he will pause, and then look at Mom. She dutifully answers for him. After two or three pauses of that sort, I'll look directly at the child and say, "Usually when I have a child who always looks to Mom before answering, or who pauses before answering, I know I have a situation where the youngest has *trained* Mom to answer for him. He knows if he waits long enough, Mom will always answer for him. That's already happened three times today. Is that what you're doing? Are you stalling on purpose because you know Mom will come to your rescue and answer for you?"

Both Mom and the kid suddenly see what's been happening. Even then the kid will look to Mom for her response, though by this time she's determined to remain quiet. Finally, the child agrees that his "training" really worked.

Age Spread Difference

Usually when four or more years separate one child from the next in line, the younger will often act like the oldest of a second set of children. Because of their spread in ages they are usually too far apart to be close and compete with each other's accomplishments.

EMOTIONAL STRESS

Experiences with Death

A child who has experienced the death of a sibling learns a lot about life. Whatever the reason for a child's death — accident, illness or birth defect — the child closest in age may feel responsible. That's due in most part to the surviving child's *normal* degree of rivalry, competition and resentment. When a child dies, what had been resentment develops into guilt that the surviving child's feelings contributed to the death.

The next child born after the death of an older child will likely be handled with kid gloves, sheltered and overly protected. Such a child is much more likely to act immaturely for his age, even more so than the usual "baby" phenomenon.

Moving

Moving can be a total disaster or it can be a blessing in disguise. The current trend shows the average child moves six times before graduating from high school. A move, especially to a different city or state can have very positive or negative effects on children's personalities. Changes and promotions in parents' jobs can cause changes in responsibilities and responses and pressures on parents. When parents change their lifestyle, their change naturally modifies the child's lifestyle, too.

Moving represents a time of starting over and devel-oping new aspects of identity and personality. Some therapists actually support moving as a *healthy* way to handle difficult problems.

Handicapped

At times handicapped children will feel like they have a giant neon sign on their heads. The sign is continually flashing "defective, defective, defective." Simply having the handicap tends to result in his receiving different parental treatment. Usually this is through over indulgence, excessive sympathy or an overly protective manner.

One of the most interesting jobs I've ever held involved rehabilitation work with visually-impaired children and adults. For three years I talked with interesting people with a variety of visual problems ranging from loss of one eye to complete blindness. Over and over I was impressed by a consistent attitude among adults who were blind. Conversation went something like this:

"Roger, you sighted people often do us blind folks a disservice by the way you treat us."

In the middle of trying to help, I felt a little defensive when I heard those words. I really felt we had all been extremely thoughtful. "How's that?" I asked.

"You often feel sorry for us and try to make things easier for us. I'll tell you something, Roger. Since they can't transplant eyes yet, the sooner a blind kid learns to walk with a cane by himself and to read Braille, the sooner he's going to accept his handicap and become independent. That's tough, but that's the way it is."

Over the years since then, it's been my experience that whenever a child's handicap can't be corrected through surgery or therapy, the sooner that child's parents help him adjust and cope with the handicap, the better off the child will be. Parents, if your child has any sort of handicap, don't intensify the problem by indulging him. The sooner he learns to live and cope with it, the better for all concerned.

HYPERACTIVE DIFFERENCES

Some kids have a stem that seems always to be wound too tight. They are just born that way. Some babies are easy, while some are average in temperament. A few are difficult and seem especially fussy; they may be prone to colic or catch every possible childhood illness, and may even be ultra sensitive to any change in their environment. Fortunately, these kinds of biological problems may disappear by the time the child reaches puberty.

What Is Hyperactive?

What about the child who may be hyperactive? One of the primary reasons I get referrals from pediatricians is suspected hyperactivity. Hyperactivity is an overused term. I have heard it used to describe anything from acting restless to neurological impairment. It's been my experience that the vast majority of children referred to me as hyperactive are, in fact, emotionally nervous but not biologically hyperactive. Understanding the difference is important because biological hyperactivity may require medical treatment, while psychological hyperactivity can usually be handled by using Common Sense Discipline techniques. There are two questions to ask yourself when you suspect a child is hyperactive:

1. "Can this child watch TV for at least 30 minutes, if it's a program he enjoys, without getting up or getting restless, except during commercials?"

2. "Is this hyperactivity present only with certain people in certain settings?"

If your answer to both questions is "No," then the child may be biologically hyperactive. But if either question is answered "Yes," the problem is likely not biological in my opinion.

Over and over I've heard parents respond to the TV question with, "Oh, if it's something he likes to watch, like Saturday morning cartoons, he can sit for two hours straight, almost without moving a muscle." I think there's little chance such a kid is biologically hyperactive. That's important, because too many parents and some physicians are too quick to put these kids on medication to control their hyperactivity.

Don't Jump to Conclusions

I've heard teachers label a child hyperactive, while other teachers describe him as typical. In such cases somebody has misdiagnosed the problem. Perhaps the teacher is the one who needs a tranquilizer, not the child.

As for those rare occasions when you answer "No" to both questions suggesting true biological hyperactivity, first check with his teachers for verification. It may be that there is only a clash of personalities between you and the child. If his teachers all report that he is hyper with them, and most of them have been using Common Sense Discipline techniques with him for at least two weeks with poor results, refer the student to the school counselor. If that doesn't help, and if the counselor concurs that the student appears hyperactive, consider having him evaluated by a qualified psychologist. Yes, he may still not be genuinely hyperactive.

For the sake of your child, have him evaluated by someone who knows how to change misbehavior with common sense methods. Remember, the majority of children referred to me with suspected hyperactivity were only emotionally nervous and responded well to Common Sense Discipline without needing to be medicated for their hyperactivity.

When a child is psychologically hyper, he is generally waving an emotional red flag that says, "Hey, look at me. I need more attention. I need help." Sometimes the hyperactivity disappears simply with additional parental attention. Someone has said that the best thing parents can give their children is time. To children, time is attention.

Hyper with a Message

Sometimes hyperactivity goes away with a bit more structure or guidelines at home. For example, some children act up because they don't know what's expected of them. This kind of hyperactivity is not physical or emotional; it's learned behavior. It's as if they have adopted the attitude, "If I just keep on testing Mom and Dad, sooner or later they'll lay down the law to me." Unfortunately, too many parents don't.

Consistency Calms Kids

Children are most calm when they know what's expected of them and what things they can do that will automatically gain parental approval. On the other hand, if they don't know what to do to get approval, or they don't know when to expect punishment, then they tend to go crazy and test the water. Here's where consistency fits in. It's easier for a child to deal with two parents who can't seem to get it together between them, than to deal with one parent who has different standards from one moment to the next. Parents and teachers should be as consistent and as predictable as possible.

PUTTING DIFFERENCES TO USE

OK, so they're different because of a number of things including birth order and biology. How can we capitalize on the differences? Proverbs 22:6 puts it this way, "Train up a child in the way he should go, and when he is old he will not depart from it." The point is that every child has a unique "way" to go. Each child is an original with a personal destiny.

If parents will look for the differences and develop the best of the differences, then they will be preparing their child for a life-long adventure with life.

First, recognize and appreciate those differences by encouraging your children to develop their individual talents. One may be better academically while another may have better musical or artistic skills. Instead of comparing them by saying, "Why aren't you good at math like your sister?" you can compliment their differences by saying, "You are each good in different areas, and that's fine with me. In school I hope you'll do as well as you can in all of your subjects."

Second, encourage your children to value each other's accomplishments. Our next-door neighbors have four children. The three boys all did well in sports, and their younger sister went with Mom and Dad to watch them play. When her piano recitals came around, Mom and Dad told her brothers they were expected to go. Like normal brothers they said, "Mom, do we have to go?"

"Yes, she went with us to watch you play, and now it's your turn to watch her play."

Third, be glad your children are different. It shows you're allowing them to grow up individually, not like cookies cut from the same mold. The more their individuality is recognized the less reason they'll have to rebel later.

DIFFERENT KIDS, SAME NEEDS

One of the most vivid descriptions of favoritism is found in the Genesis 37 story of Joseph and his eleven brothers. Born when Jacob was an old man, Joseph was the next to youngest son. He was his father's favorite and was singled out for special attention by Jacob's gift of a fancy, one-of-a-kind robe. Jacob's favoritism proved to be Joseph's undoing. His brothers began resenting him for the special attention, and finally they arranged to get rid of him. Joseph was sold into slavery.

After years of Egyptian bondage, Joseph rose in rank in the Egyptian court until he became the second highest administrator in the land (Genesis 41:40). When famine hit Canaan, Jacob sent his sons to Egypt to buy grain. Unknown to them at first, their once-hated brother became their source of hope. God took what they did out of resentment and turned it into something he meant for good.

This story has an important message for parents — don't play favorites, especially when there are stepchildren or half brothers involved. While it's natural to feel special toward one's youngest child, the older children still have their need for attention, especially as they go through the difficult teenage years. If you have stepchildren, don't try to take the place of their other parent. You will never be the natural parent. It's normal to feel more love, at least at first, for your biological children. Still, you can make the effort to give each child individualized time and attention.

A father came to see me because of the trouble he was having getting along with his teenage stepson. The boy moved with his mother and sister into the house the man had owned for a number of years. Right away the stepson felt out of place, especially since his stepfather had two older sons who were already well-established in the neighborhood.

"What can I do to make him like me?" the father asked me. "Right now, he can't stand me."

I talked to the father and learned that his job required him to go to different locations, calling on customers and seeing if equipment repairs or adjustments were needed.

"When your own kids were younger," I asked him, "did you ever take them with you on service calls?"

"Sure, all the time on weekends and when school was out."

"Okay, here's what you do. Next time you have a service call to make, ask him if he'd like to go along."

"What if he says he doesn't want to go or thinks I'm trying to butter him up?"

"Oh, he probably will at first, so expect it; but say something like you thought he might be interested in going along to see what you do or just for the ride."

As expected, the stepson balked at first. "Why me? Do I have to?"

"No, just thought you might like to." Then the stepfather wisely added, "Bill and Jack enjoyed going with me when they were your age, and I thought you might have fun coming along too."

At first the stepson avoided going, and his stepfather was discouraged at being rebuffed. I encouraged him to keep asking because the message was bound to get through eventually. Sure enough, on the third invitation, the boy jumped at the chance, and a healthy relationship was born.

In a newly blended stepfamily, it's normal for stepchildren to feel out of place. They may act edgy and on the defensive as they feel their way around. Be patient with them, offer them support and love, but don't expect them to accept you at first. They're only testing you. Stay with it, and you'll probably be rewarded by their acceptance. A family is no place to play favorites.

When you get serious about raising responsible children, it's important to invest time in understanding each child's differences. The birth order differences, unique life experiences, special problems and hyper energy levels can become strengths. If we can view these differences as strengths instead of weaknesses or defects, we will be influential in helping our children take advantage of their differences. And, helping our children in this task is what Common Sense Discipline is about.

12

Rules and Resources

Rules are like winter clothing. If you put them on all at once, especially before it's necessary, you can smother. Just as it's easy to make a young child frustrated from too many layers of unnecessary clothing, it's easy to lay on too many rules that aren't necessary. Few parents or teachers will need all of these rules. Some definitely will not apply to your children, so use your judgment.

MAKING RULES THAT WORK

To be effective rules must be

- ☐ Simple—Kids must be able to repeat them and understand them.
- ☐ Firm—Rules are not bent by a flimsy excuse.
- ☐ Fair—They are applied equally to all children.
- ☐ Flexible—They can be adjusted to fit the circumstances.

Rules are like fences. They need to be firm and strong to do the job for which they're intended, but they also need to be flexible in case something unexpected happens. Don't forget some kids require more rules than others; that's just the way kids are.

HOMEWORK RULES

1. After school, no TV until homework's done.
2. I won't do homework for you, but I'll help if you don't understand.
3. If you miss an assignment, you can call a friend or your teacher to get the assignment.
4. If you fall behind, you will have to study on weekends.
5. I expect you to earn your grades without cheating.
6. No telephone calls while you are studying, unless it's about the assignment.
7. If you need me to drive you to the library for extra resources, I'll be glad to if you give me enough advance notice.
8. You are responsible for remembering your assignments and keeping up with your materials and books.

RULES FOR MEALS

1. Come to breakfast after you have dressed and taken care of your room.
2. Be polite about seconds. Ask if others would like something else first.
3. You may have dessert after you have eaten an appropriate portion of your meal.
4. When we finish our meals, we all rinse our plates and put them in the sink/dishwasher.

5. After a meal, everyone helps by clearing the table and putting away leftover food.
6. When you make a snack, you are expected to clean up after yourself.
7. You are responsible for serving your friends snacks while they are here and for cleaning up any mess they might make.
8. Because you are part of the family, you are expected to share in the chores of cooking, cleaning up and putting away groceries.
9. We only eat in the kitchen or dining rooms.

RULES ABOUT PETS

1. You are responsible for feeding your pet.
2. Your pet needs regular attention and play times.
3. You will be expected to bathe your pet and clean its house/cage when I tell you it's appropriate.
4. If you fail to take care of your pet, then I may sell it or give it to another child who will provide better care for it.

RULES ABOUT GIFTS

1. When someone gives you a gift, you always write a "thank you" note before using the gift.
2. I will be happy to help you word a "thank you" note if you first get the paper and pencils.

RULES ABOUT PHONE CALLS

1. On school nights, if your homework is finished, you may use the phone until 9:00 pm.
2. There are to be no phone calls after 9:00 pm. If someone calls you after that time, I'll take a message.

3. If you tie up the phone for more than 15 minutes at a time, you may lose your phone privileges for the next day.

BEDTIME RULES FOR PRESCHOOLERS

1. I will tuck you in bed once and read a story.
2. If you can't sleep, you are welcome to look at books or play quietly so long as you stay in bed and you don't disturb the rest of us.
3. After you brush your teeth for the night, no more snacks.
4. Once you go to bed, you are welcome to get all the water you want, but you will have to get it yourself.

RULES FOR TV

1. No TV in the mornings on school days. On weekends, no TV until you've had breakfast and picked up your room.
2. No TV in the evenings until you've completed all your homework.
3. If the TV is too loud, I'll ask you once to turn it down. If the sound remains too loud, you will have to turn the TV off for 30 minutes.
4. You may watch only those shows we agree on ahead of time and that we've circled together on the TV news.

CLASSROOM RULES

1. Because we recognize our collective responsibility to this class we will arrive on time, in an orderly fashion, ready to participate and study.
2. We will behave in a polite and considerate manner that permits each one to study and learn.
3. We will respect each person's right to dignity. Negative remarks about one's family, birthplace, race or

religion will be considered insults and are inappropriate at school.

4. We will respect each other's property. We consider the school building(s), equipment and grounds our collective property.

5. We will earn our grades fairly and honestly with dignity. We will not brag or ridicule about grades.

6. Exceptional behavior in this class will be recognized appropriately. Students with excellent grades and those with exceptional improvement will be acknowledged. Students whose actions detract from the learning environment can expect to receive consequences in front of the class.

7. We will accept our responsibility to encourage and correct each other when necessary.

8. We will apologize when appropriate.

9. We recognize that violations of these rules will be subject to consequences set by our school's district administrators, teachers and our class's Student Disciplinary Committee (Note: This may be an ad hoc committee).

(Permission granted to recopy the above list for noncommercial classroom use only with this designation: "Reprinted by permission from *Common Sense Discipline: What to Say and Do When Kids Need Help*, © 1986, available from Sweet Publishing, 3934 Sandshell, Fort Worth, TX 76137.")

WHAT TO TELL YOUR KIDS ABOUT SEX

Consider the following chart as a guide to appropriate times to discuss various aspects of sexuality. Helping children to understand their sexuality will build their confidence.

Age	Concepts To Teach	Opportunities
3-6 years	Identify body parts, using correct names Talk about when it's the best time to discuss our bodies (at home, not in public) Talk about where babies come from and how they grow	Newborns Play house
6-8 years	Teach modesty and self-respect Privacy, nudity	Playing doctor Questions/bathroom/ showers Newborns Words/jokes
8-10 years	Explain conception Respond to questions and make opportunities to talk even if there are no questions Discuss the problems with vulgar talk Help kids learn to control emotions Use social events as a lab for testing modesty and appropriate language Prepare for body changes Pornography	Awareness of parents making love Visiting a baby TV Films/movies Books about body

10-15 years	Share times when you had a crush on someone	Talks
		TV
		Movies
	Teach how to make value decisions/saying "no"	Practice decisions
		Books
		Group dating
	How to draw the line	God's view of "why wait?"
	Assure the awareness of developmental time clock	Magazines
		Books, discussion
	Talk about hormones and their effect on sexual desire/affection	
	Talk about desire coming from God/natural and good	
	Demonstrate effect and appropriate hugging in front of kids	
	Teach relationship of sex and marriage	
15-18 years	Talk about how people use sex to manipulate	TV
		Movies
		Magazines
	Help them learn to set limits	Discussion stories
		One-on-one talks
	Ask some "what if" questions	

MONEYMAKING IDEAS FOR TEENAGERS

1. Entertaining at birthday parties: dress like a clown and put on a magic or puppet show. If you play an instrument, be sure to play "Happy Birthday" as the cake is brought out. Either puppet or magic shows can earn you $10-15 for a 15 to 30-

minute performance. Parents appreciate someone who can take charge, so be prepared with some fun games for the children. Balloon stomp is a fun game where each child receives a balloon and a piece of string about 2 feet long. After blowing up the balloon, tie one end of the string to the balloon and the other to your foot. All guests stand in a circle, each with his balloon tied to his foot. At "go," everyone tries to stomp and break the others' balloons while keeping his intact. Each time a balloon breaks that person has to sit down and is given a piece of bubble gum to start chewing for a bubble-blowing contest. The last person left with a balloon gets a prize. Then he joins in the bubble-blowing contest. Give prizes for biggest bubble, smallest, longest-lasting and messiest.

2. Serving and cleaning up at parties can earn you money. The biggest hassle for most adults who give parties for their friends or children is the cleanup afterwards. Arrange with one or two other responsible teens to offer to set up tables, fill guests' glasses with tea or coffee, and clean up afterwards, washing, drying and putting away dishes.

3. Trimming trees and shrubs and mowing yards are always good moneymakers. If you're willing to work fast and hard, you'll do best by working "by the job" rather than by the hour. Then, the faster you work, the more you make.

4. Wash, wax, and clean cars using fabric and vinyl cleaners.

5. Water plants while owners are away.

6. Recycle aluminum cans.

7. Repair and paint fences.

8. Wash windows. Ask your mom for her advice of cleaning solutions. Some people recommend polishing with old newspapers crumpled up. They're easy to obtain and cheap.
9. Clean houses, vacuum, and clean out garages and basements.
10. Walk or sit with dogs.
11. Distribute leaflets for small businesses.
12. Tutor students.
13. At Christmas time you can earn money by removing mistletoe from trees, breaking it into small clumps with lots of berries, tying a red ribbon bow on each clump, and selling them door to door. Putting the clumps into plastic sandwich bags will help protect them and keep them fresh looking.
14. Children's Day Out: For the standard baby-sitting fee in your neighborhood, offer to take several children to a local park or zoo for an outing. Be sure you have another teen along for help, and charge extra if you provide a lunch or snack. Keep your outings to an hour or an hour and a half at first while you get the hang of this. Require small, preschool children to walk holding onto a rope with one teen as the leader and a partner at the back to watch for problems or falls.
15. Take photos at birthday parties with an instant camera.

Other Helpful Resources

Adams, Caren, Jennifer Fay and Jan Loreen-Martin. *No Is Not Enough: Helping Teenagers Avoid Sexual Assault*. San Luis Obispo, CA: Impact Publishers, 1981.

Adams, Caren and Jennifer Fay. *No More Secrets: Protecting Your Child From Sexual Assault*. San Luis Obispo, CA: Impact Publishers, 1984.

Barlett, Eleanor, Dorothy Ging and Charles Herndon. *God Made Us: About Sex and Growing Up*. Nashville, TN: Graded Press, 1980.

Curran, Dolares. *Traits of a Healthy Family*. Minneapolis: Winston Press, 1983.

Dads Only Newsletter, P.O. Box 340, Julian, CA 92036.

Dobson, James. *Dare To Discipline*. Wheaton, IL: Tyndale House Publishers, 1973.

Elkind, David. *The Hurried Child: Growing Up Too Fast Too Soon*. Reading, MA: Addison-Wesley, 1981.

Focus on the Family Newsletter, P.O. Box 500, Arcadia, CA 91006.

Gardner, Richard. *The Boys and Girls Book About Divorce*. New York: Bantam Books, 1971.

———. *The Boys and Girls Book About One Parent Families*. New York: Bantam Books, n.d.

———. *The Boys and Girls Book About Stepfamilies*. New York: Bantam Books, 1985. (See page 121.)

———. *The Parents' Book About Divorce*. New York: Bantam Books, 1979.

Grollman, Earl. *Talking About Death*. Boston: Beacon Press, 1976.

Kavanaugh, Dorriet. *Listen To Us*. New York: Workman Publishing, 1978.

Ketterman, Grace. *How to Teach Your Child About Sex*. Old Tappan, NJ: Revell Company, 1981.

Lickona, Thomas. *Raising Good Children*. New York: Bantam Books, 1983.

Norman, Jane and Myron Harris. *The Private Life of The American Teenager*. New York: Rawson, Wade Publishing, 1981.

Practical Parenting Newsletter. 18326B Minnetonka Blvd., Wayzata, MN 55391.

Rambo, Lewis. *The Divorcing Christian*. Nashville: Abingdon, 1983.

Rekers, George. *Growing Up Straight*. Chicago: Moody Press, 1982.

Scott, Sharon. *Peer Pressure Reversal*. Amherst, MA: Human Resource Development Press, 1985.

Self-Therapy for the Stutterer. Memphis, TN: Speech Foundation of America, 1981.

Wilson, Earl. *You Try Being a Teenager*. Portland, OR: Multnomah Press, 1982.